BLACK RAINBOW OVER OEDIPUS AT THEBES LOBSTERS FISHING M
EN EROTIC BLANDO FRUTO THE FLYING DUTCHMAN GLORIA SE
NTINEL SIGHTING DOWN I MARKER WHIPPET MARAUDER THE C
HARIOT OF DARIUS II NAVY SIGHTING DOWN II PORT CLYDE DRE
AMSCAPE OUR ROOM, TENSING PENN JAMAICA JA
MEN THROUGH THE BINOX WIGWAM GLORIA I CO
SCAPE EL PALENQUE EROTIC BLANDO FRUTO: LA
CANO ARENAL YZ FALLS JAMAICA BLACK RAINBOW OVER OEDIP
US AT THEBES LOBSTERS FISHING MEN EROTIC BLANDO FRUTO T
HE FLYING DUTCHMAN GLORIA SENTINEL SIGHTING DOWN I M
ARKER WHIPPET MARAUDER THE CHARIOT OF DARIUS II NAVY S
IGHTING DOWN II PORT CLYDE DREAMSCAPE OUR ROOM, TENSIN
G PENN JAMAICA JAMAICAN FISHERMEN THROUGH THE BINOX W
IGWAM GLORIA I COSTA RICA ROCKSCAPE EL PALENQUE EROTIC
BLANDO FRUTO: LA MARIPOSA VOLCANO ARENAL YZ FALLS JAM
AICA BLACK RAINBOW OVER OEDIPUS AT THEBES LOBSTERS FISHI
NG MEN EROTIC BLANDO FRUTO THE FLYING DUTCHMAN GLORI
A SENTINEL SIGHTING DOWN I MARKER WHIPPET MARAUDER T
HE CHARIOT OF DARIUS II NAVY SIGHTING DOWN II PORT CLYDE
DREAMSCAPE OUR ROOM, TENSING PENN JAMAICA JAMAICAN FI
SHERMEN THROUGH THE BINOX WIGWAM GLORIA I COSTA RICA
ROCKSCAPE EL PALENQUE EROTIC BLANDO FRUTO: LA MARIPOSA
VOLCANO ARENAL YZ FALLS JAMAICA BLACK RAINBOW OVER OE
DIPUS AT THEBES LOBSTERS FISHING MEN EROTIC BLANDO FRUT
O THE FLYING DUTCHMAN GLORIA SENTINEL SIGHTING DOWN I
MARKER WHIPPET MARAUDER THE CHARIOT OF DARIUS II NAVY
SIGHTING DOWN II PORT CLYDE DREAMSCAPE OUR ROOM, TENSI
NG PENN JAMAICA JAMAICAN FISHERMEN THROUGH THE BINOX
WIGWAM GLORIA I COSTA RICA ROCKSCAPE EL PALENQUE EROTI
C BLANDO FRUTO: LA MARIPOSA VOLCANO ARENAL YZ FALLS JA
MAICA BLACK RAINBOW OVER OEDIPUS AT THEBES LOBSTERS FIS
HING MEN EROTIC BLANDO FRUTO THE FLYING DUTCHMAN GLO
RIA SENTINEL SIGHTING DOWN I MARKER WHIPPET MARAUDER
THE CHARIOT OF DARIUS II NAVY SIGHTING DOWN II PORT CLYD
E DREAMSCAPE OUR ROOM, TENSING PENN JAMAICA JAMAICAN F
ISHERMEN THROUGH THE BINOX WIGWAM GLORIA I COSTA RICA
ROCKSCAPE EL PALENQUE EROTIC BLANDO FRUTO: LA MARIPOSA
VOLCANO ARENAL YZ FALLS JAMAICA BLACK RAINBOW OVER OE
DIPUS AT THEBES LOBSTERS FISHING MEN EROTIC BLANDO FRUT
O THE FLYING DUTCHMAN GLORIA SENTINEL SIGHTING DOWN I
MARKER WHIPPET MARAUDER THE CHARIOT OF DARIUS II NAVY

ANTHONY d'OFFAY GALLERY
LONDON 1990

MALCOLM MORLEY

A DANCE OF PAINT, A DANCE OF DEATH

David Sylvester

You can turn away from the canvas to look at something else and still be assailed by the paint as if particles of it were being propelled in every direction. Even as its energy seems to fill the room, its surface seems somehow to remain immaculate. Moreover, the image presents vertiginous spaces which behave like vortices, yet the surface still seems flat and solid as a slab of marble. The work is a paradigm of contained violence. It always has been with Morley, but the polarity becomes increasingly assertive.

*

Morley is very much an international artist, perhaps in rather the same way as de Kooning. Any self-respecting professional observer coming to the work for the first time would expect to be able to tell that it was painted in New York and by a European hand; he would hope to be able to tell that the hand in the one case was Dutch, English in the other. At the same time, Morley's language is peculiarly inclusive. His handling of paint seems full of quotations from or reminders of a wide variety of twentieth-century painterly painters — Pollock, de Kooning, Nolde, Kokoschka, Matisse, early Rouault, mid-20s Soutine (those large red areas in the recent work which seem to be Madeleine Castaing's dress).

The packing-in of masses of figurative detail means that the brush-work often evokes that of past masters: Constable's large oil-sketches come to mind; so, in all his flashiness, does Lawrence. The other day,

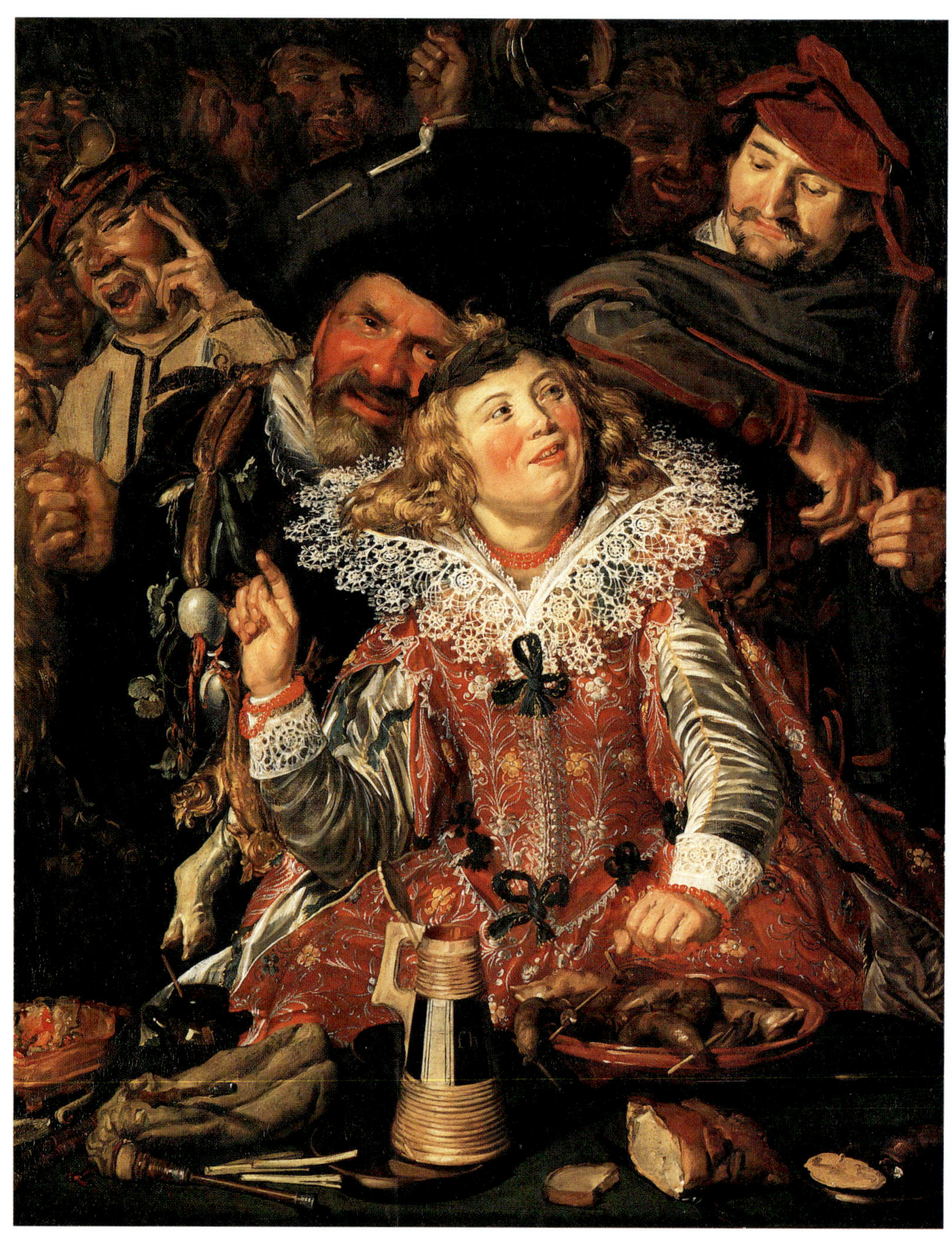

Frans Hals, *Merrymakers at Shrovetide*, c. 1615. Oil on canvas, 51¾ x 39¼ inches.
Courtesy Metropolitan Museum of Art, New York, bequest of Benjamin Altman.

in the Metropolitan Museum, I was made to think of Morley by Frans Hals's picture of a mardi gras revel. I remembered having long ago compared this work with de Kooning's Women pictures, but that had largely been to prove a point about de Kooning's rootedness in a Dutch tradition; Morley's affinity is more comprehensive. A rearing mass of faces, lewd looks, grimacing mouths, bawdy gestures, diverse genital metaphors, thrusting movement in all directions, white impasto for the lace and the parallel pleats along the arms in a reddish dress, a mood — save in the character at top right, who has everything under control — of Dionysian fever, a Falstaff at the centre of the action, at the periphery an assortment of fleshy faces, ubiquitous ambiguities in the performance and the roles including the likelihood that the girl is a boy, pleasure pursued frantically, chaos come again.

*

Like the work of, say, Magritte or Jasper Johns, Morley's has been haunted by objects belonging to his boyhood. With Magritte such objects include reading primers, stereoscopic images, paper cut-outs, masks, metal puzzles, printed puzzles, comic strips, adventure books; with Johns, targets, flags, numbers, lettering, rulers, balls, maps; with Morley, tin soldiers, toy weapons, model airplanes, model ships, books about warfare (picture books but also things like the Biggles books) and the Coronation Mug which was handed out to school-children at the time of the crowning of King George VI. Morley was six, and he says that the decoration of this mug has been the source of his idea of colour.

His Rosebud, lost to him when destroyed in an air raid on London, was a painted balsa wood model he made of a famous warship, his favourite among several such models. It has come back, it appears, in one of the sculptures he has lately started making — a grey model of a battle cruiser mounted on a tall grey oval plinth which stands for the ocean and succeeds in evoking its depth and somehow in suggesting its perils. Like most of the eight sculptures Morley has made so far, it strongly relates in its sense of deliquescence and concomitant threat of loss to Medardo Rosso and to Giacometti. These sculptures also relate to Giacometti's, of course, in the ways in which image and base are inseparable.

Giacometti told me that he found tin soldiers in shop windows more relevant to reality than most contemporary figurative sculpture. Morley's sculptures mostly recall toy soldiers or their tanks or guns. They deal, it seems to me, with two sets of feelings experienced in boyhood. There is the feeling of attachment to certain objects which is stronger than any admitted feeling about human beings and which therefore produces acute anxiety or desolation about the fear or reality of their loss. And there is the feeling as puberty comes of the frightening force of one's growing virility together with its antidote, the identification of objects which resemble the irrepressible member in an entertaining way. Morley's two images of machine-gunners are splendidly potent symbols of this sort. The sculptures are reminders that toys are our education in the facts of death and life.

*

'What is fascinating now,' Francis Bacon said in 1962, 'is that it's going to become much more difficult for the artist, because he must really deepen the game to be any good at all.' Morley is one of the few who seem to be deepening the game, which means, of course, always playing for high stakes. He invests exceptional technical resources in pushing pictorial languages to ridiculous extremes. Above all, his involvement in a pursuit to their limits of the drama and desperation of existence drives him as if without fear to explore the frontiers of madness.

*

He is not lighthearted in his use of ancient myths. Most modern artists, including Picasso, seem to be using the myths, as, say, Boucher did, as a pretext for making art of a certain sort. Morley seems to be using

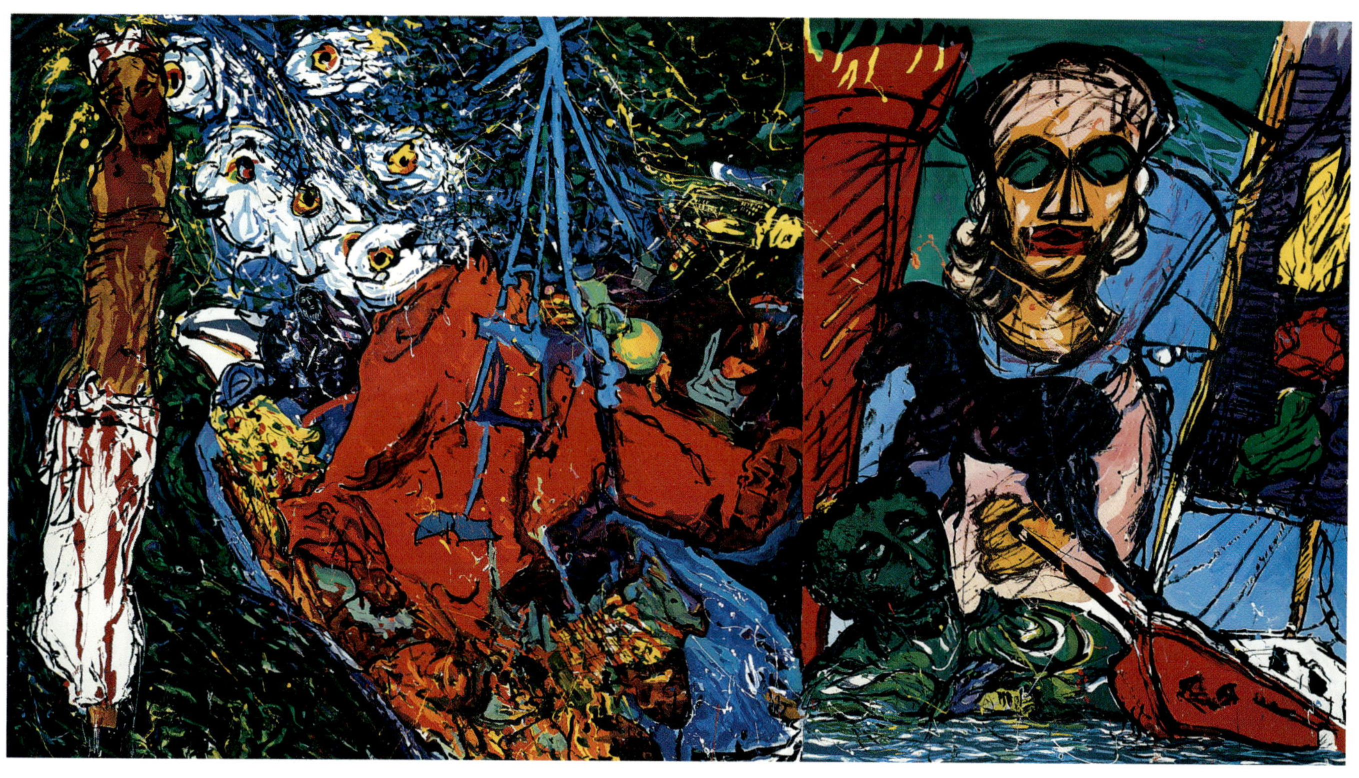

Malcolm Morley, *Aegean Crime*, 1987. Oil and wax on canvas, 78 x 159¼ inches.
Private collection, courtesy The Pace Gallery, New York.

his art to brood upon the myths. He gives them both weight and immediacy, in a fashion which I find very reminiscent of Max Beckmann. He conveys a feeling that those were titanic days. He seems to have some urgent inner involvement with the stories to inspire the iconography he invents for them, full of new ironic conceits — for example, in that tremendous dance of death, *Black Rainbow over Oedipus at Thebes*, the way the letters in the Greek inscription across the base of the image are spaced so that they look like letters in a card for testing eyesight.

That was done knowingly. Other things done unknowingly are even more relevant to my point. I was looking for the first time at another picture on the same scale painted a year earlier and called *Aegean Crime*. I recognised the characters from other works as being based on sculptures from which Morley had made drawings in various museums, the figure on the left being, he said, a French Romanesque Christ, the head at top right Minoan and the bust at bottom right a Roman copy of a bust of Alexander the Great. After looking at the picture for some time, awed by its atmosphere of tragedy, menace and revenge, I thought about the title and started asking myself what the subject could be. The clue seemed to be in the head at top right, its eyes veiled by a venomous green and therefore perhaps the blinded eyes of another Oedipus image. But there was too much going on that suggested a different interpretation. That dominant figure must be Clytaemnestra with a baleful gaze and the bearded head below her of a man largely submerged in water must be Agamemnon slaughtered in his bath; the Christ-like figure would be a symbol of sacrifice, while the two boats in the picture would represent, first, Agamemnon's fleet becalmed until he offered his daughter up for sacrifice, second, the vessel which brought him back to his bloody end. It was all as obvious and inevitable as the solution to a crossword clue once it is found. When I next saw Morley I congratulated him on his portrayal of Agamemnon and Clytaemnestra. Politely he told me that he could not remember having heard of them. Three cheers for the collective unconscious.

SHOWING THE VIEW TO A BLIND MAN

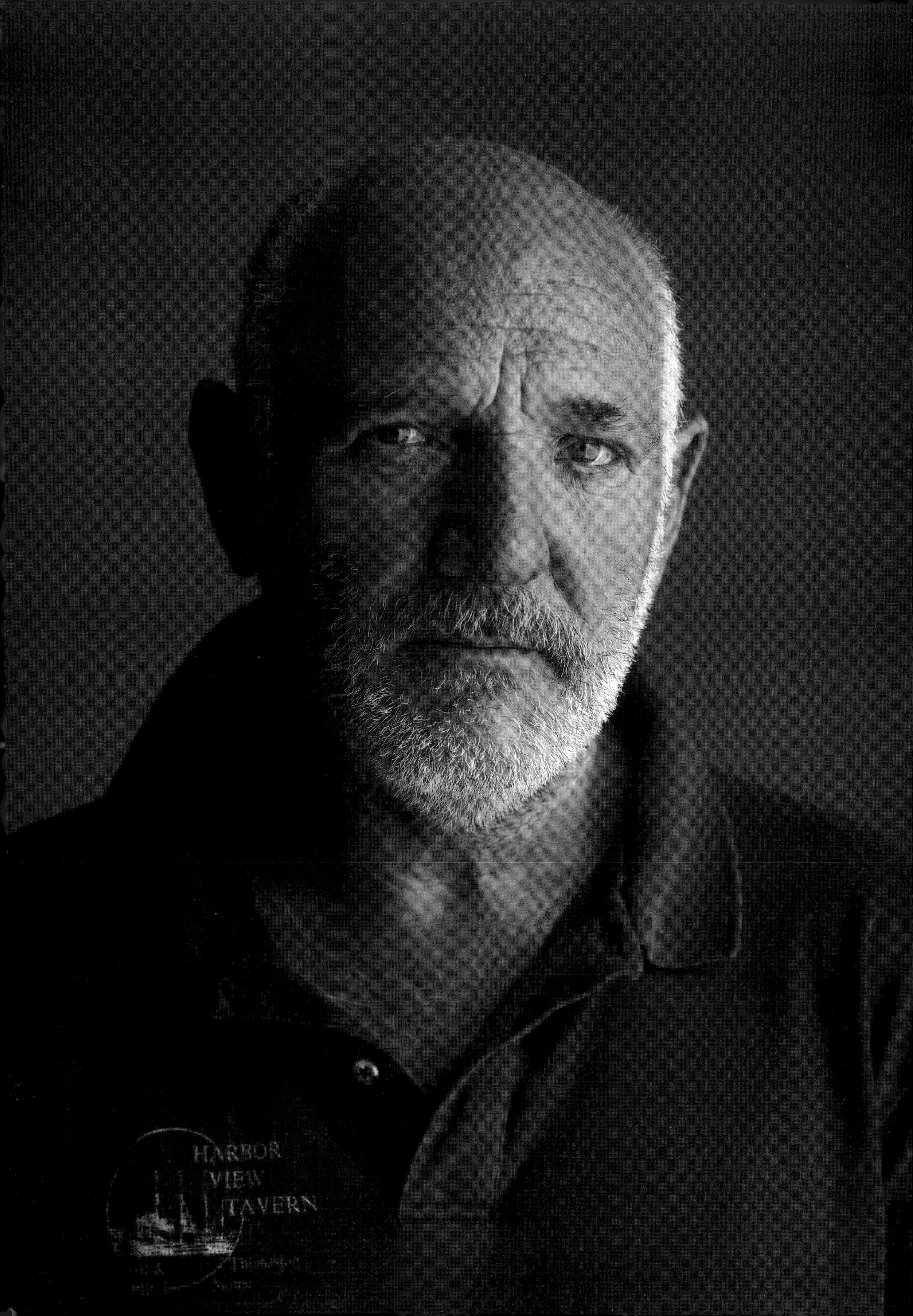

HARBOR
VIEW
TAVERN

SHOWING THE VIEW TO A BLIND MAN

Malcolm Morley talking to David Sylvester

SEEING THE WORLD GREY

Colour is such an emotional thing. One of Piaget's tests on children's perception of colour showed that children whose parents were divorced saw less colour. They literally saw things greyer, and children who came from a happy family literally perceived colour as being brighter. And I remember myself seeing the world grey. I could not see colour in the world for many years as a young painter.

SHOWING THE VIEW TO A BLIND MAN

I've been writing a film script for ten years. It's the story of Thomas, Thomas the painter. And it's a saga from World War II to the present time, a sort of cultural *War and Peace* with the social history of New York thrown in, with a complete reconstruction of the Cedar Bar.

It has a lovely metaphor on seeing for the modern artist. When I was a little boy my grandmother took me to the seaside at Folkestone and we were walking along the boardwalk and it was the most beautiful day, with sailboats sailing by, billowing white clouds, stuff like that. I must have been about six or seven. And I went up to a man sitting on a bench and tugged at his coat and said, Oh! Look at the ships, look at the ships, aren't they nice! And he said to me, Can you read, sonny? And I said, Yes, I can read. And he said, Can you read what's on this button? And it said, BLIND. And at that moment my grandmother came up and grabbed my hand and said, Can't you see he's blind? I wanted to disappear completely.

And that's a metaphor of myself as an artist, to show the view to a blind man. I have that in the film script. Thomas is in a sailor suit. I've got that indelibly in my mind. The man is wearing black glasses and the reflection of the boats is on his glasses but he's not able to see them. *Black Rainbow over Oedipus at Thebes* is a metaphor for blindness.

BLACK RAINBOW OVER OEDIPUS AT THEBES

The Oedipus painting looks like brown shit. I think this brownness is rather disconcerting, but I love the idea which Barney Newman, who was my great teacher really, gave me that in Hebrew the word for Adam and Earth is the same word. That just blew me apart.

The origins of this painting are extraordinary. One is a little drawing that I made in Greece at the theatre at Epidaurus, at a performance of *Oedipus Rex*. A most fantastic experience even without knowing a word of Greek, and I was riveted. For the chorus they have a whole regiment of modern army soldiers, about a thousand, dressed up as ancient Greeks, coming over the hill. And you know that they have been walking over this hill for three thousand years, the same spot, the same rock. Oedipus looks as if he's made of stone, with his eyes gouged out. It's just fantastic. Anyway, I made this drawing and I made a lithograph from it which I used for part of this painting. And I took the rainbow from another watercolour that I made in Africa over Mount Kenya. The three figures below are local people who have a boat here in Bellport.

Then it was very important to me to make the title. The work of putting on the lettering was damned difficult because I had to use stencils. I wanted these letters to float, saying in Greek, Black Rainbow over Oedipus at Thebes. I couldn't tell you why, but I love the sound of it, the way it comes off your mouth. The titles are very important to me. It would be very interesting if you just took all the titles of the paintings and made a poem from them, without anything else.

BEAUTIFUL GROUND STROKE, BY GOD!

I only want to paint in oil paint on canvas, not in oil paint on oil paint. I'm not an oil painter on oil paint, I'm an oil painter on canvas. And I must have that ground all the time to paint upon. It feels horrible when I start to paint on top of paint which is still drying underneath at different levels, with skin on top.

I once had this idea of starting a magazine called *Oil Painting*. It wouldn't discuss anything else, and a critic would write in the way a sports writer would write when looking at tennis. He would say, Beautiful ground stroke, by God, look at the way he stroked that, and in that yellow, that Naples yellow!

WHAT OIL PAINT WANTS

You could make oil paint function in a transparent fashion, but you would have to alter the material of it. Oil paint functions more power-fully, more effectively, if you are using it in terms of its own nature. It does not want to be thinned down. Watercolour wants to be thin. I think that all of the work I do is very involved in what the nature of the material itself is.

PAINTER AND SCULPTOR

The painter looks at the landscape and paints it. Does the sculptor look at the landscape and sculpt it?

SNOWSTORM IN WASHINGTON SQUARE

When I was making my ugly pictures, ugly from the idea of doing something for yourself that you've never seen before, I used to throw up at the end of each picture, in front of it. It was so appallingly horrible and it was so appallingly true. It took me seven years to be able to look at them. Now I think they're beautiful. I've got some that are really insane, these paintings, shapes like equilateral triangles, cutting triangles out of the grid and looking at them. I was very involved with Buckminster Fuller's 60 degree thing and going out into nature to paint through these holes. In fact I was once in the Village doing it. It was in a snowstorm and I was painting a snowman in the middle of a snowstorm in Washington Square. I had this triangular painting with a triangle cut out of it in the middle of the grids, which were triangular. So I'm looking through this triangle and an eye comes through and says, My God, it's Malcolm! And it was Cy Twombly and Rauschenburg and a whole gang of people just wandering around in the snow. It was kind of embarrassing, a guy out in the snow with an equilateral triangle looking like some kind of witch.

PLEASURE

Why do I paint? I do it to get pleasure. But I'm not easy to please. So it becomes a sort of carrot.

BLEEDING EYES

Cézanne said that he felt his eyes bleeding when he took them off one object to the next. Can you imagine that idea? It's Oedipus again, of the bleeding eyes. You can imagine the idea of the eyes sucking, like a suction pad. I feel like that myself sometimes, that the eye sucks onto this and that it hurts to let go and move on to the next place.

PAINTING AS A HEARTBEAT

I have this theory about smoking and the heartbeat of the mother —
that in the womb, maybe, you're hearing the heartbeat and that the
impulse towards repetition, for example, masturbation or compulsive
smoking, anything repeating itself, is an assurance of that original
heartbeat neurotically sustained. It's just the neurosis of repetition
in itself, it almost doesn't matter what is being repeated. Artists fall very
quickly into the idea of repetition and compulsion as a form of security.

BREATHING OUT IS GETTING LOST

Often, when making a painting, there's some kind of resistance, and it
changes from picture to picture. In one instance it might be the resistance
of the canvas that doesn't feel quite good, that you don't have quite the
right ground. Or another is the resistance that you don't have the right
balance in the medium. Another resistance is that the brushes aren't
quite right, etc, etc. And for years the next picture would be a kind of
plan to try to solve the problem of resistance in the last picture. After
many years I found out that it didn't matter what you did. I decided
that the resistance was just self-consciousness in doing something and
that, to use Norman Brown's lovely phrase, the way to true happiness
was to get lost.

It works like a pulse, getting lost or not getting lost. Almost to a degree
of inhalation and exhalation. Breathing in is being self-conscious and
breathing out is getting lost. When I've self-consciously mixed some
paint I can go and get lost until I've used up that material. Then I mix
it again. So I have spurts of getting lost and of being very aware of myself
as a doing creature throughout the paintings as they happen.

I've made friends with my resistance, it's no longer my enemy.
I don't battle on through no matter what. I stop and ask what it is.
For example, I couldn't paint *Gloria* after a while. Then I realised there

was too much to look at and I covered most of the canvas with brown paper and started in a new place. I only had a little white canvas left to look at and I was able then to proceed; I had lowered the resistance. There had been so much input coming from what I had previously painted that it was slowing down the painting of new areas, so I concealed from myself what I had done before. I have to paint in a way like a typist typing a manuscript and not knowing at the end how it reads.

THE WHOLE THING IN NEW YORK

The whole thing in New York when I came here was that you had to do something new that hadn't been done before. But everything you do has been done before one way or another. All those stripes, they're all in Renaissance painting —in little corners. The history of newness in art resides in looking at the left hand corner of previous painting and blowing that up. You take a de Kooning and blow that up and you get field painting. You could take a detail out of any of these early Renaissance paintings and you've got beautiful modernistic art.

PAINTINGS

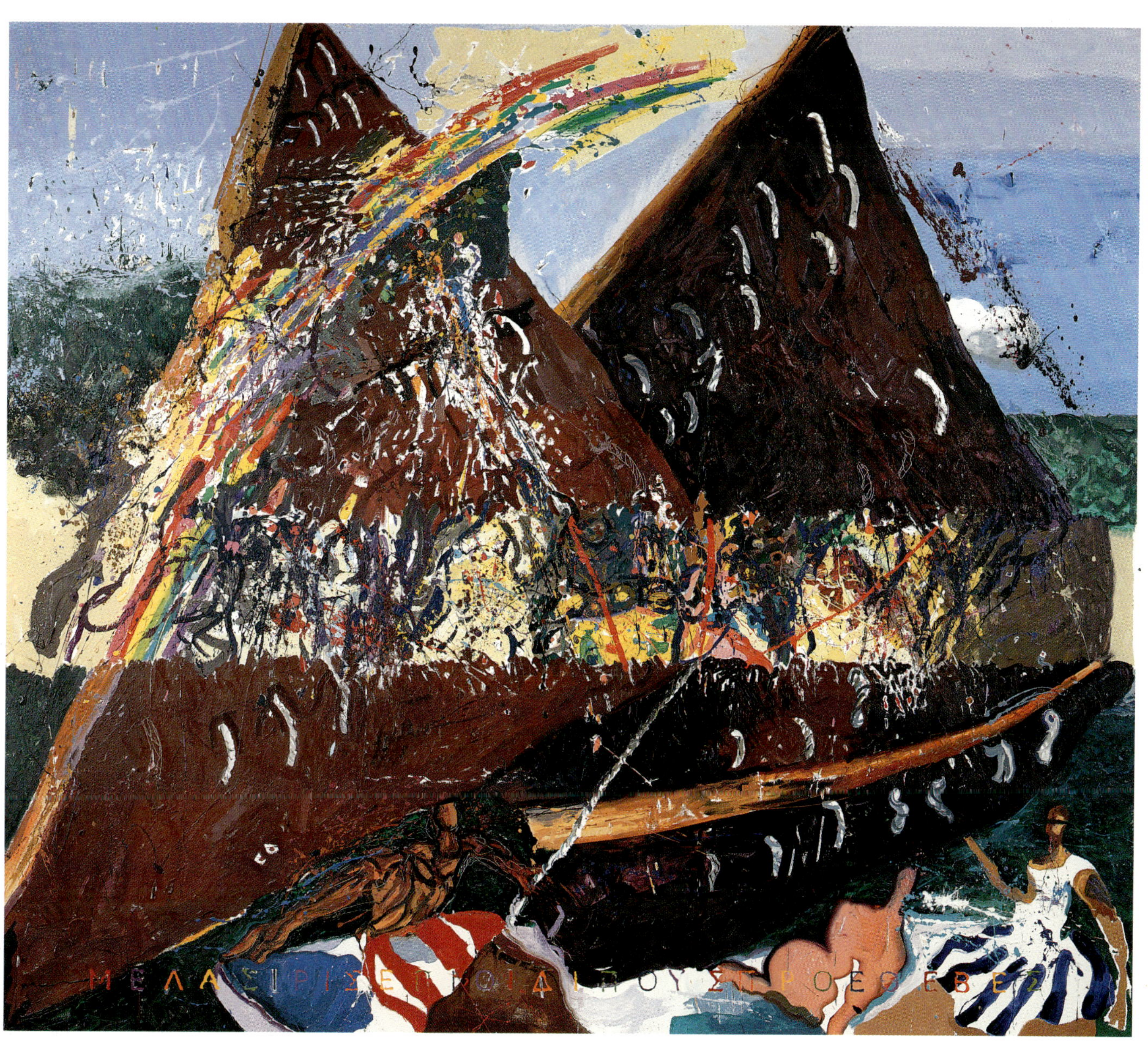

Black Rainbow over Oedipus at Thebes
1988
Oil and wax on canvas
114 x 127 inches

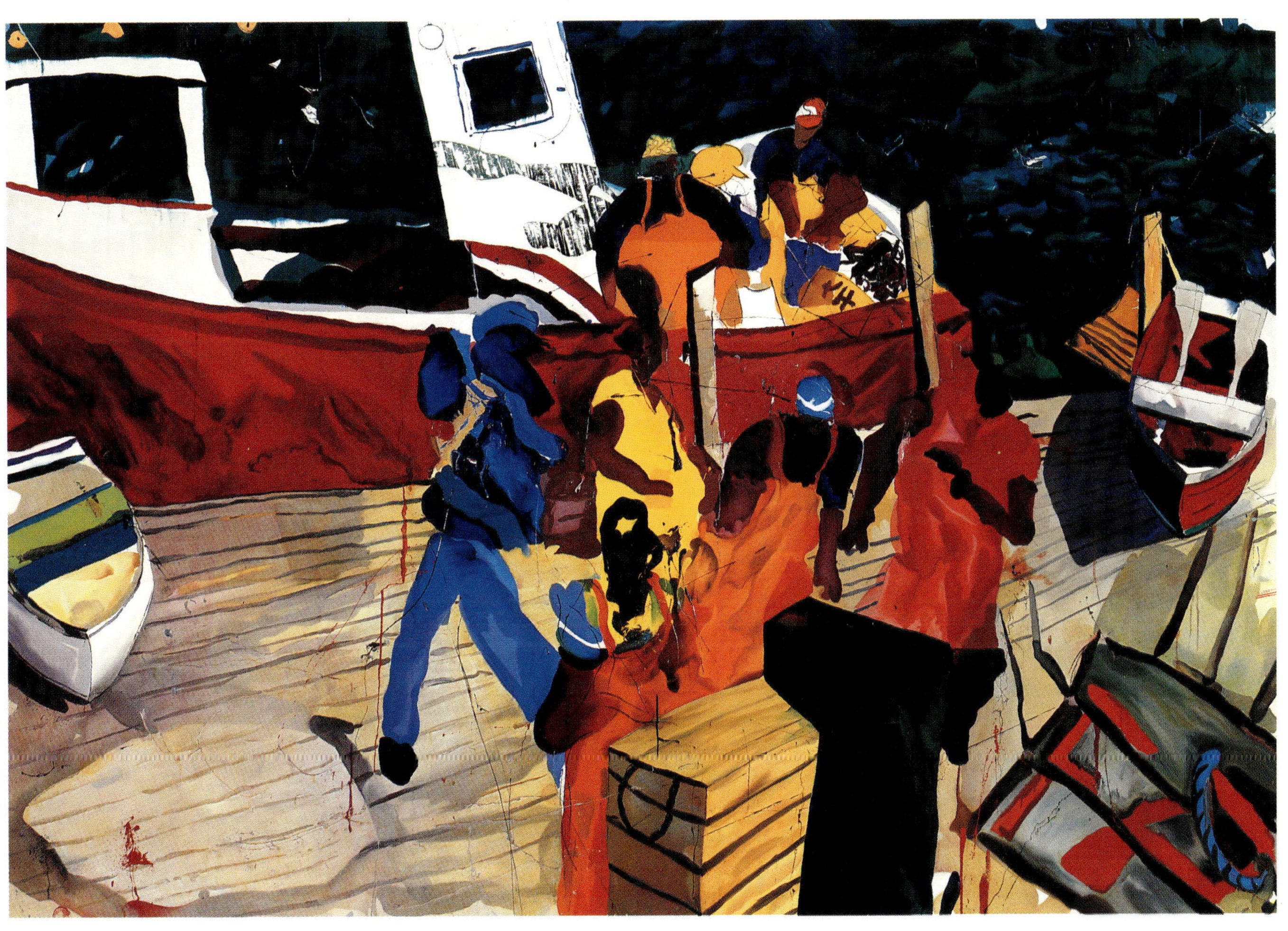

Lobsters Fishing Men
1989
Oil on canvas
78½ x 110½ inches

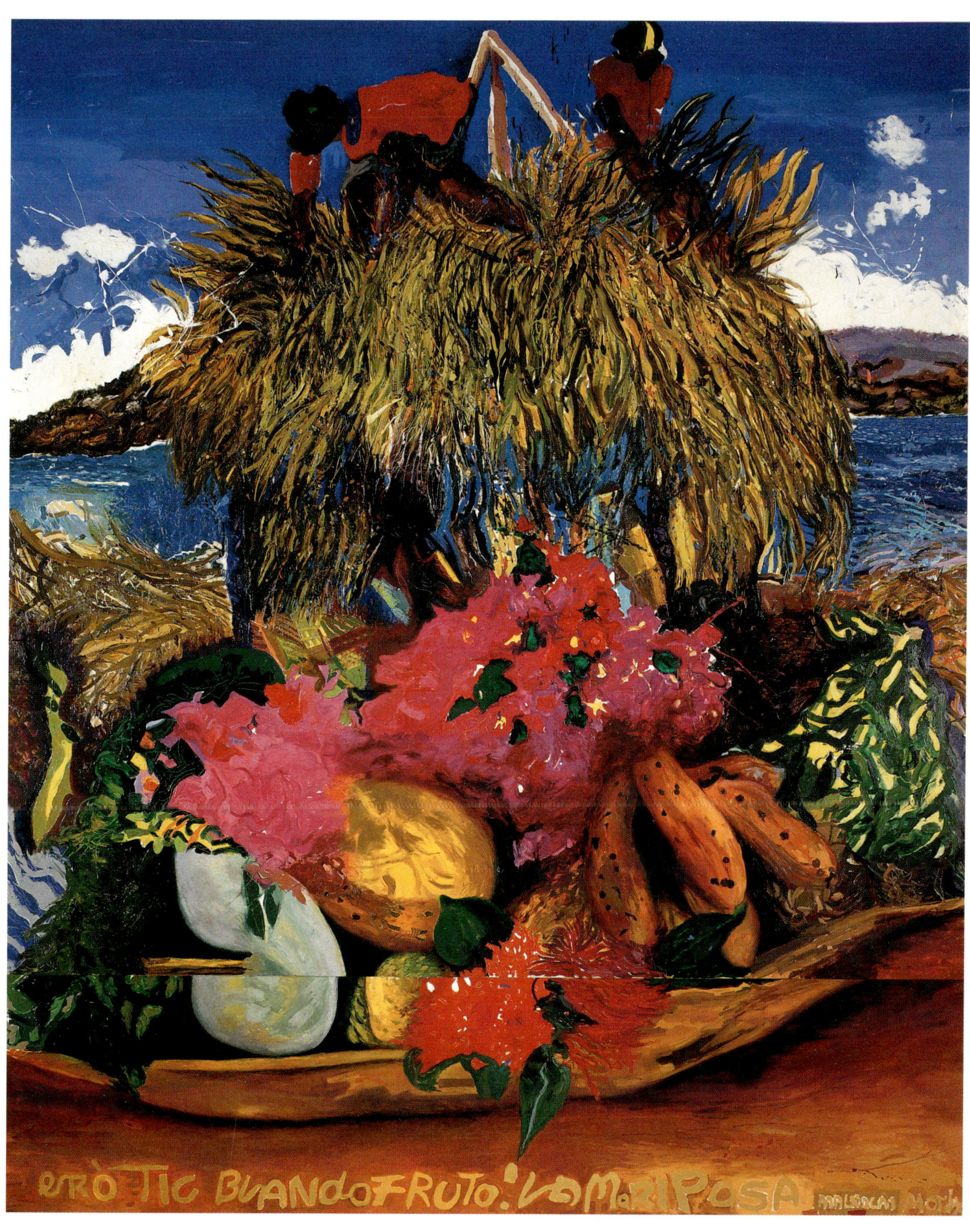

Erotic Blando Fruto
1989
Oil on canvas
133¾ x 107¾ inches

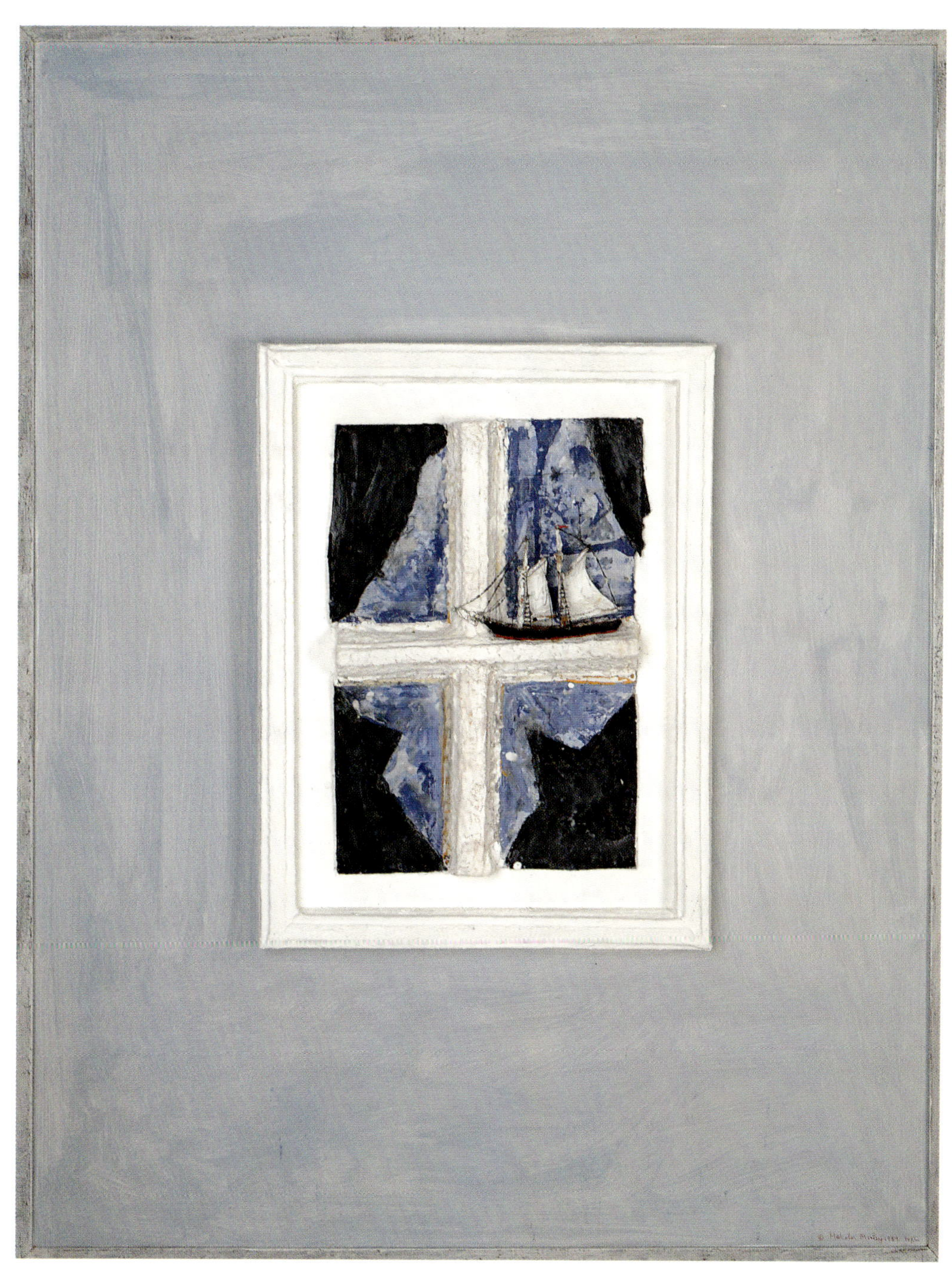

The Flying Dutchman
1990
Encaustic on panel
55¾ x 41½ x 4 inches

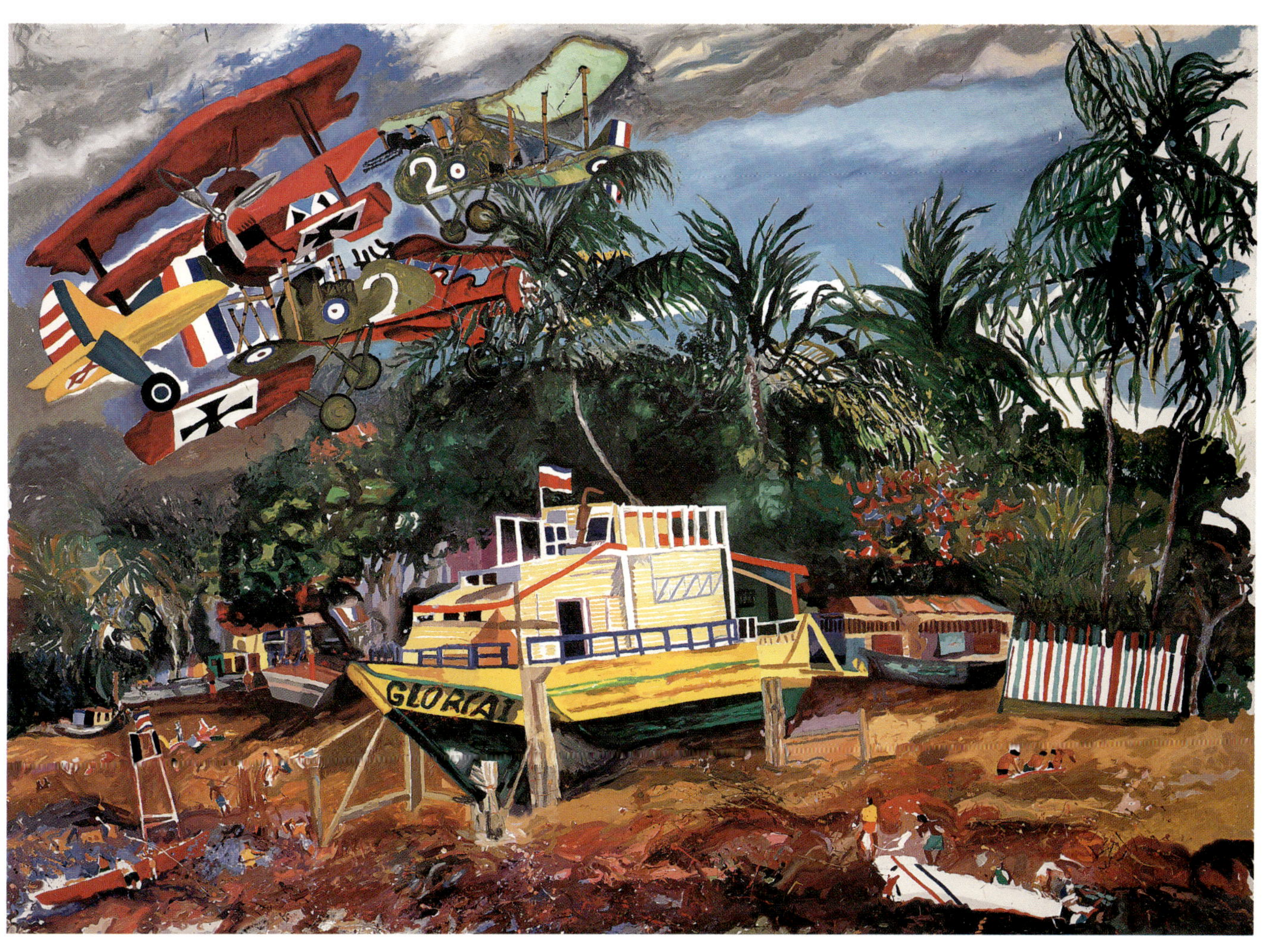

Gloria
1990
Oil on canvas
92 x 124 inches

SCULPTURE

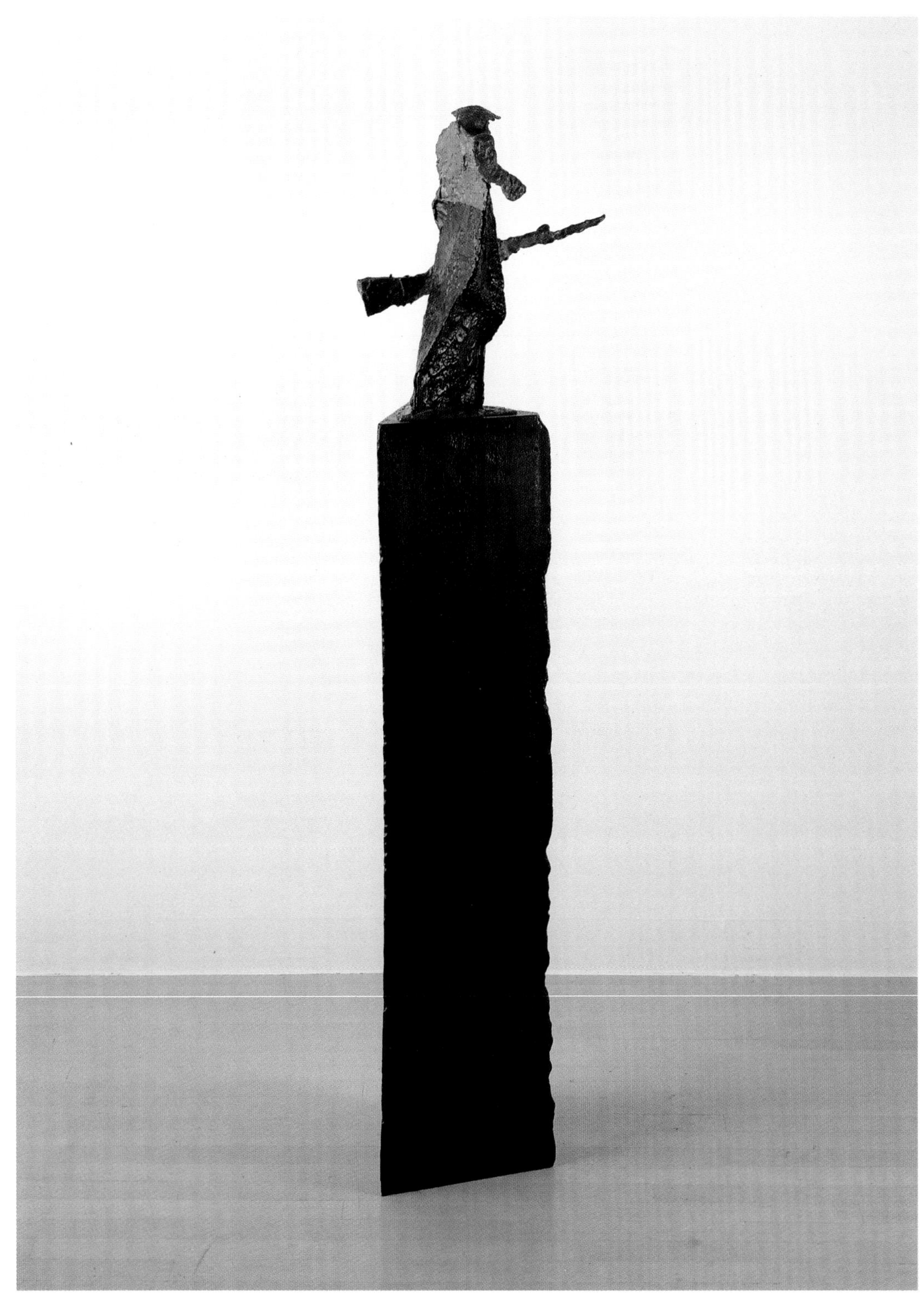

Sentinel
1989
Patinated bronze
69 x 11 x 11 inches
Edition of six

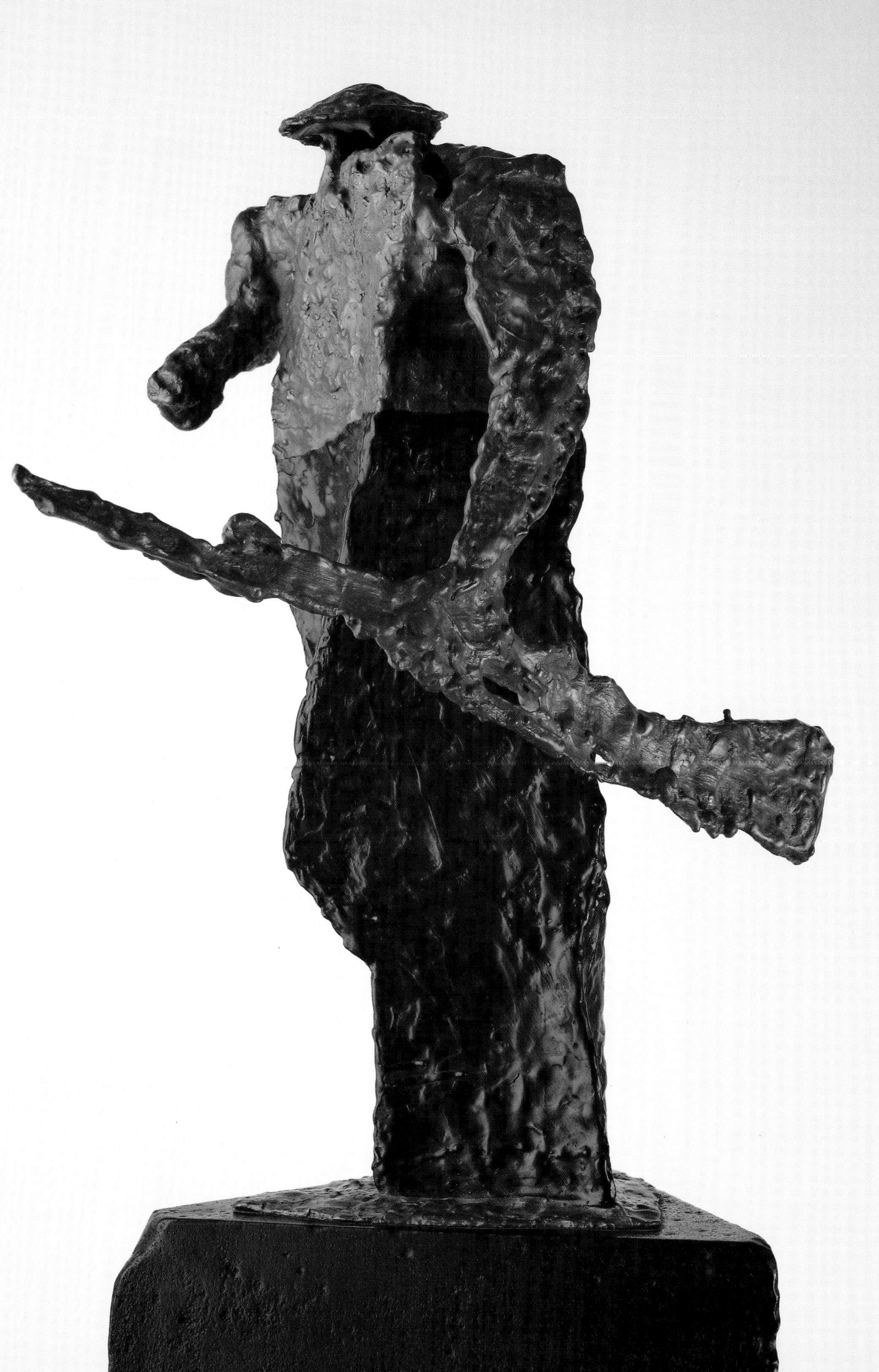

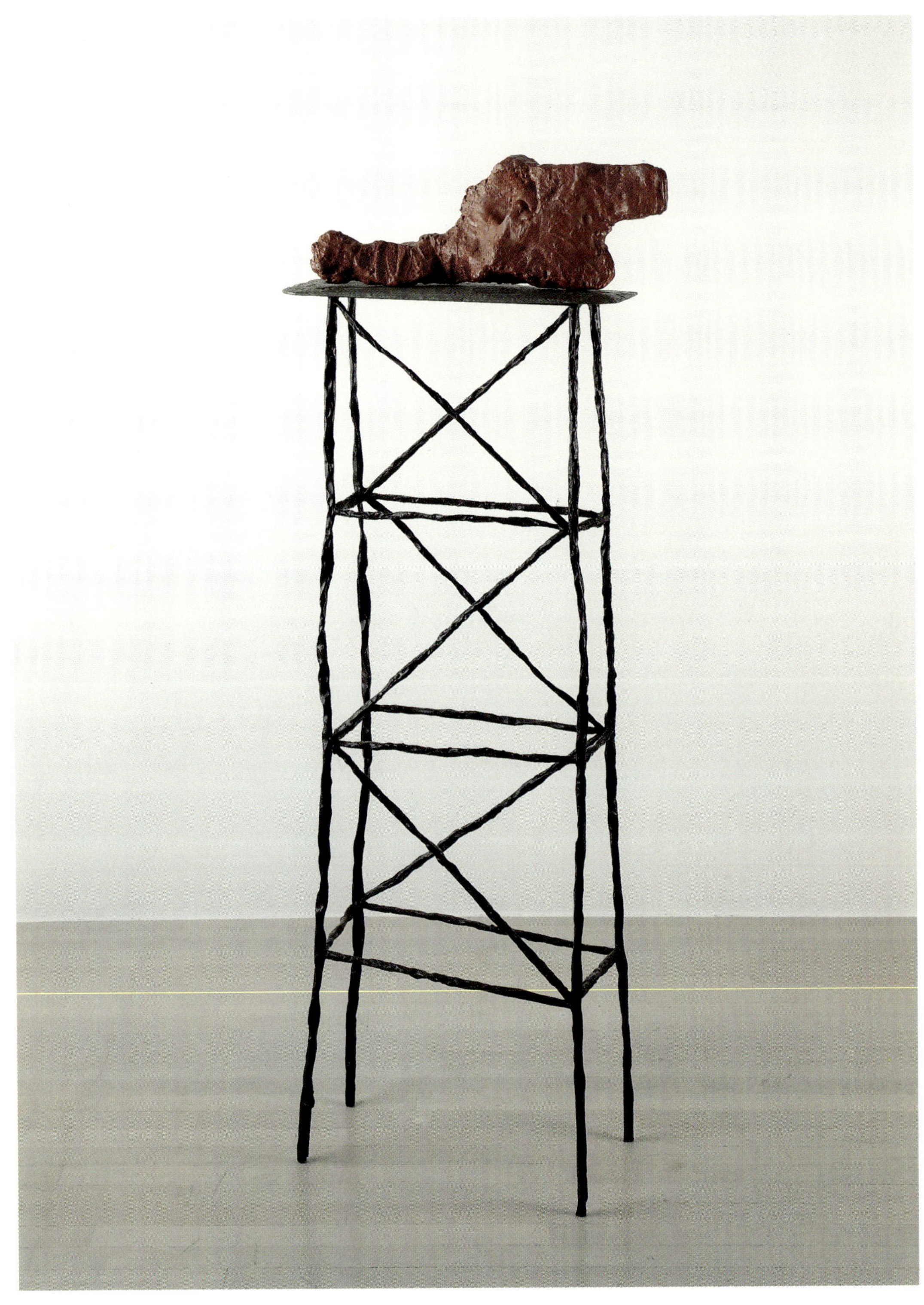

Sighting Down I
1989
Patinated bronze
60 x 19 x 16 inches
Edition of six

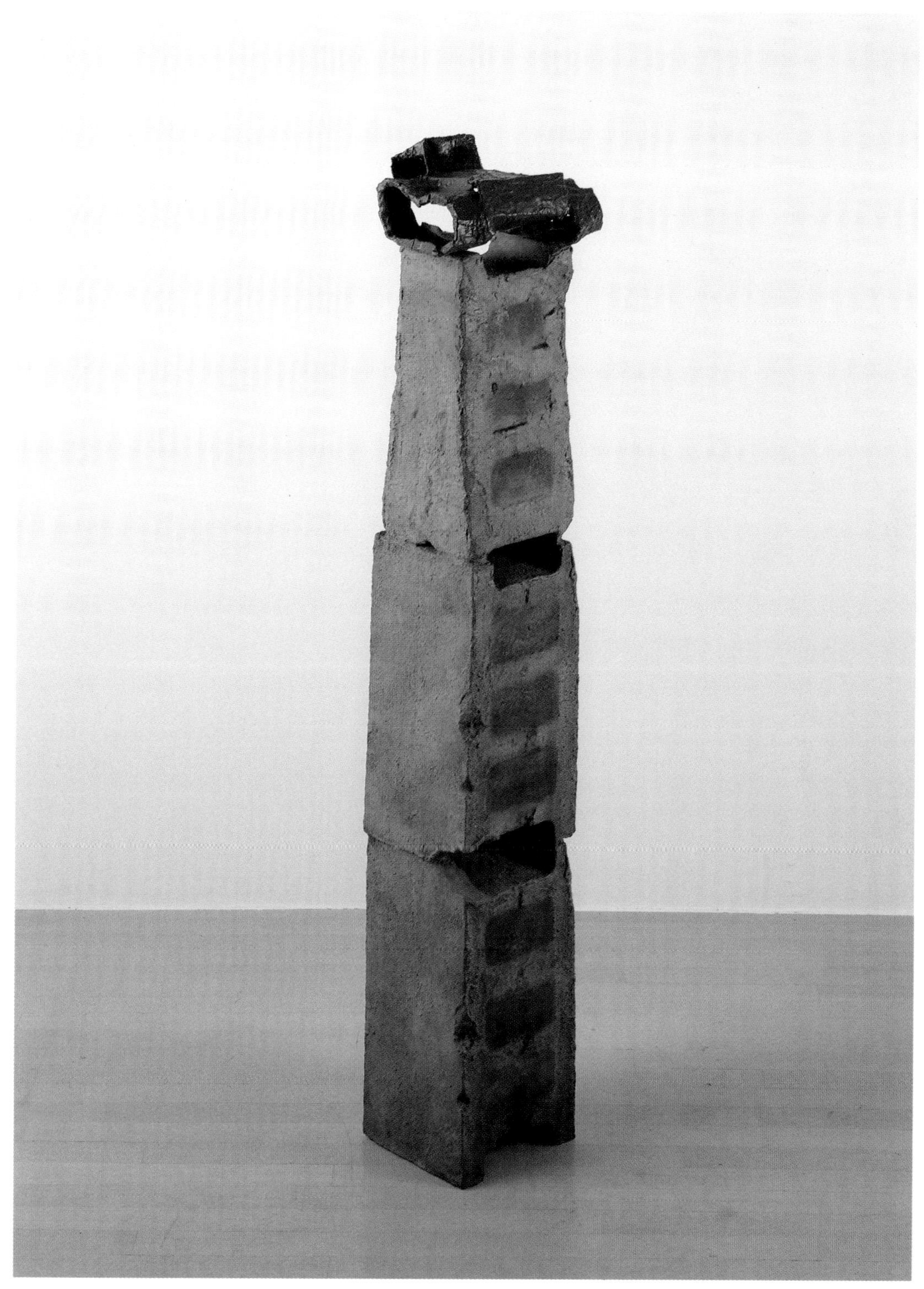

Marker
1989
Patinated bronze
51¾ x 10½ x 11 inches
Edition of six

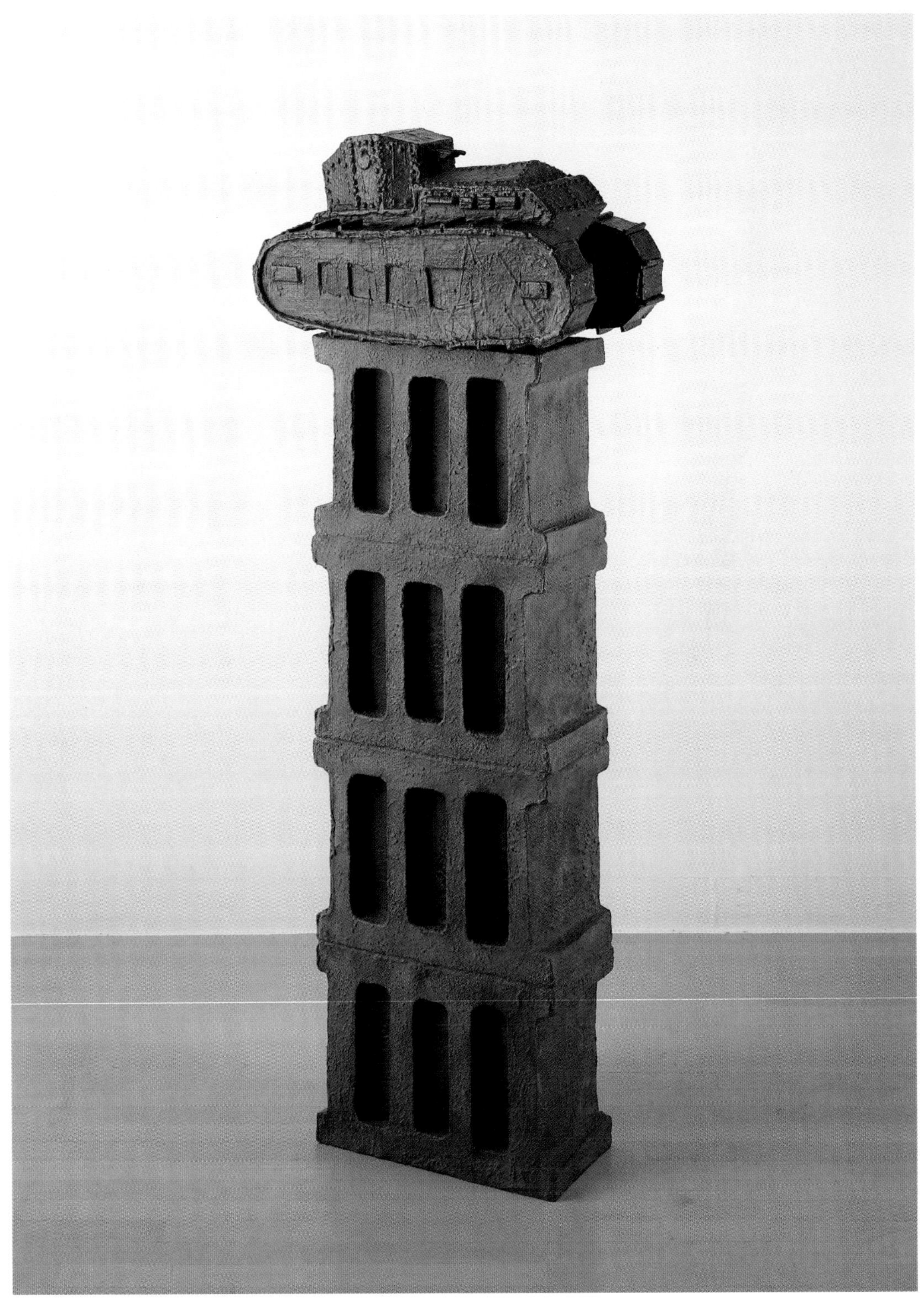

Whippet
1989
Patinated bronze
58½ x 22½ x 11 inches
Edition of six

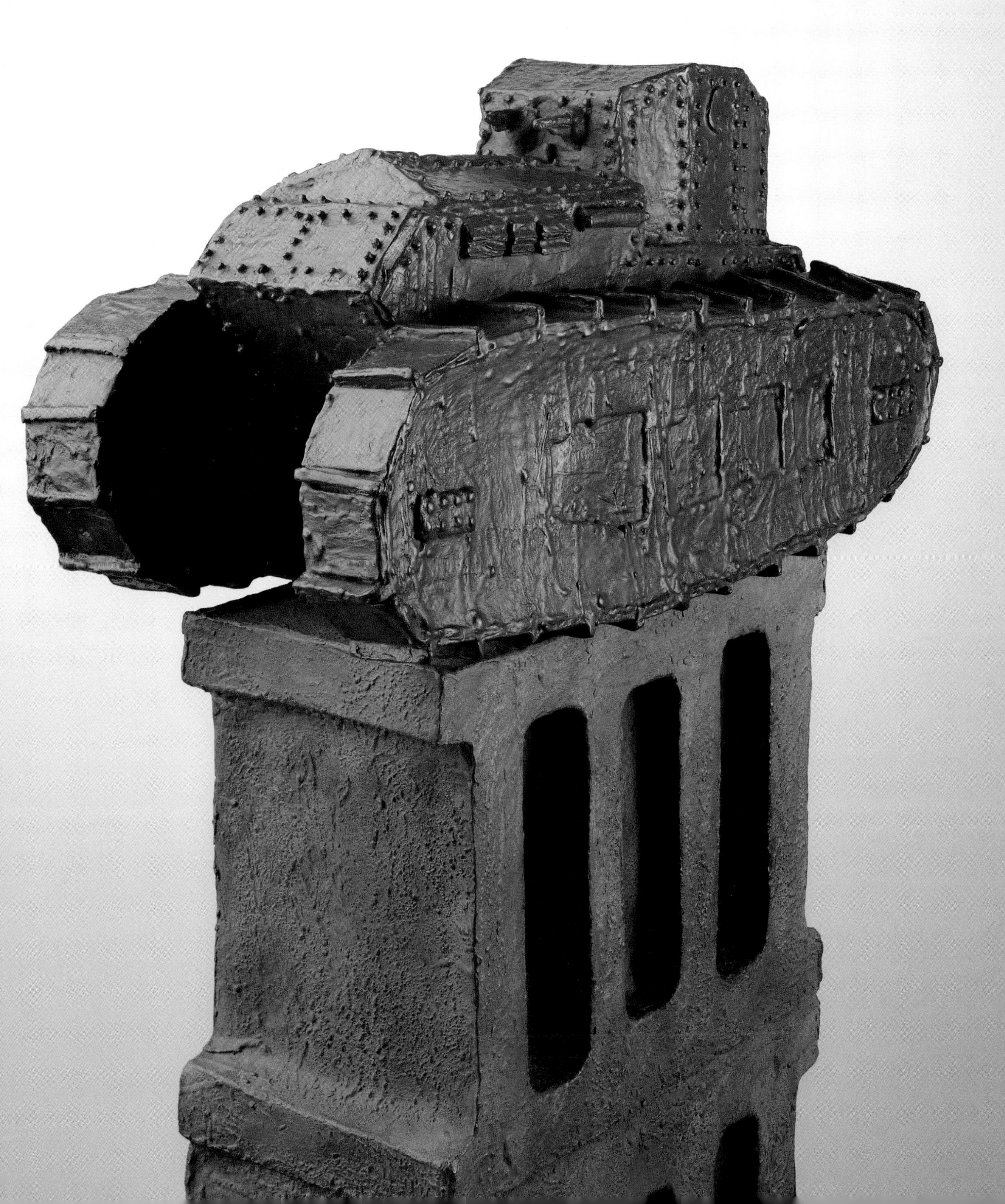

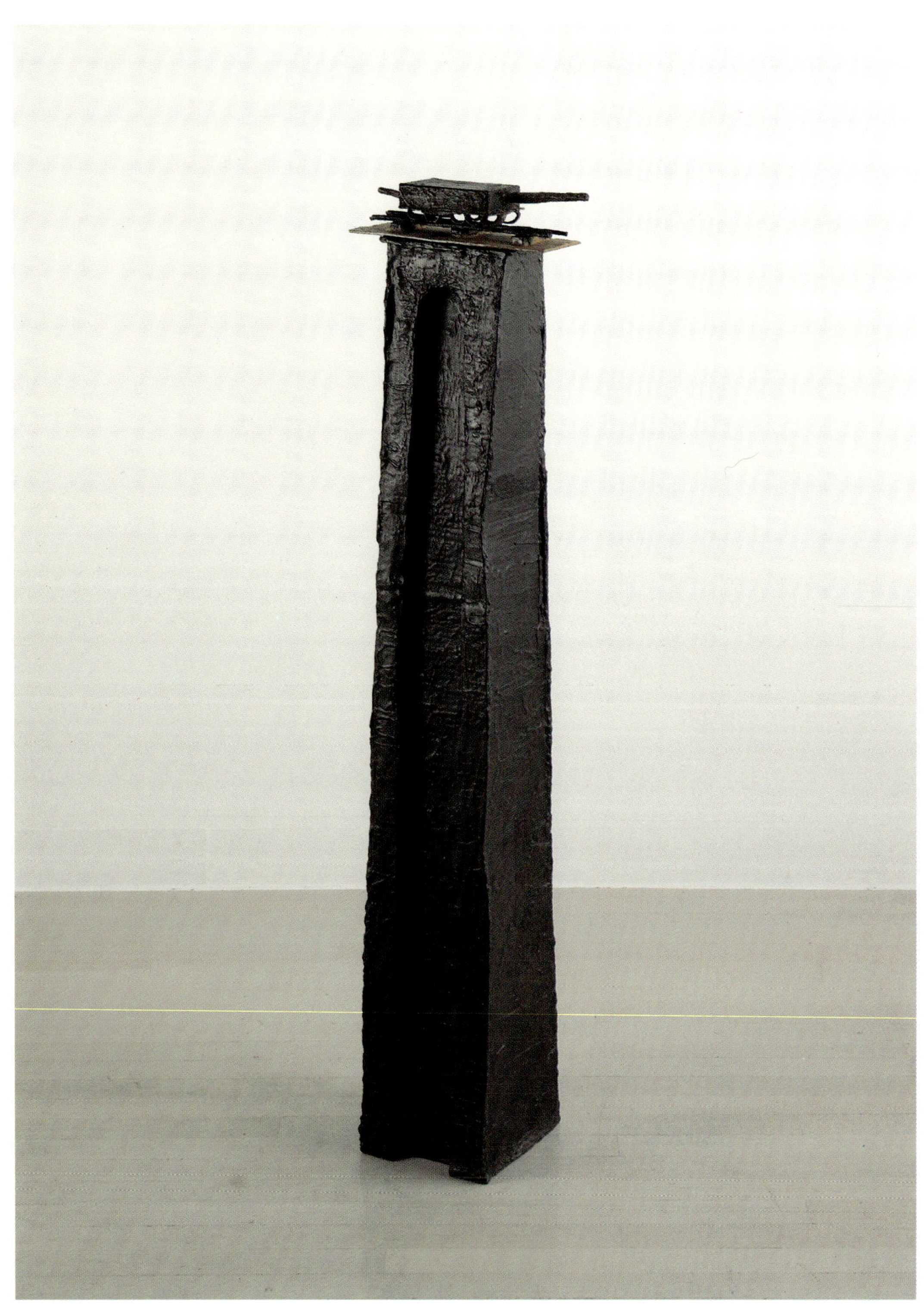

Marauder
1989
Patinated bronze
50 x 15 x 8¼ inches
Edition of six

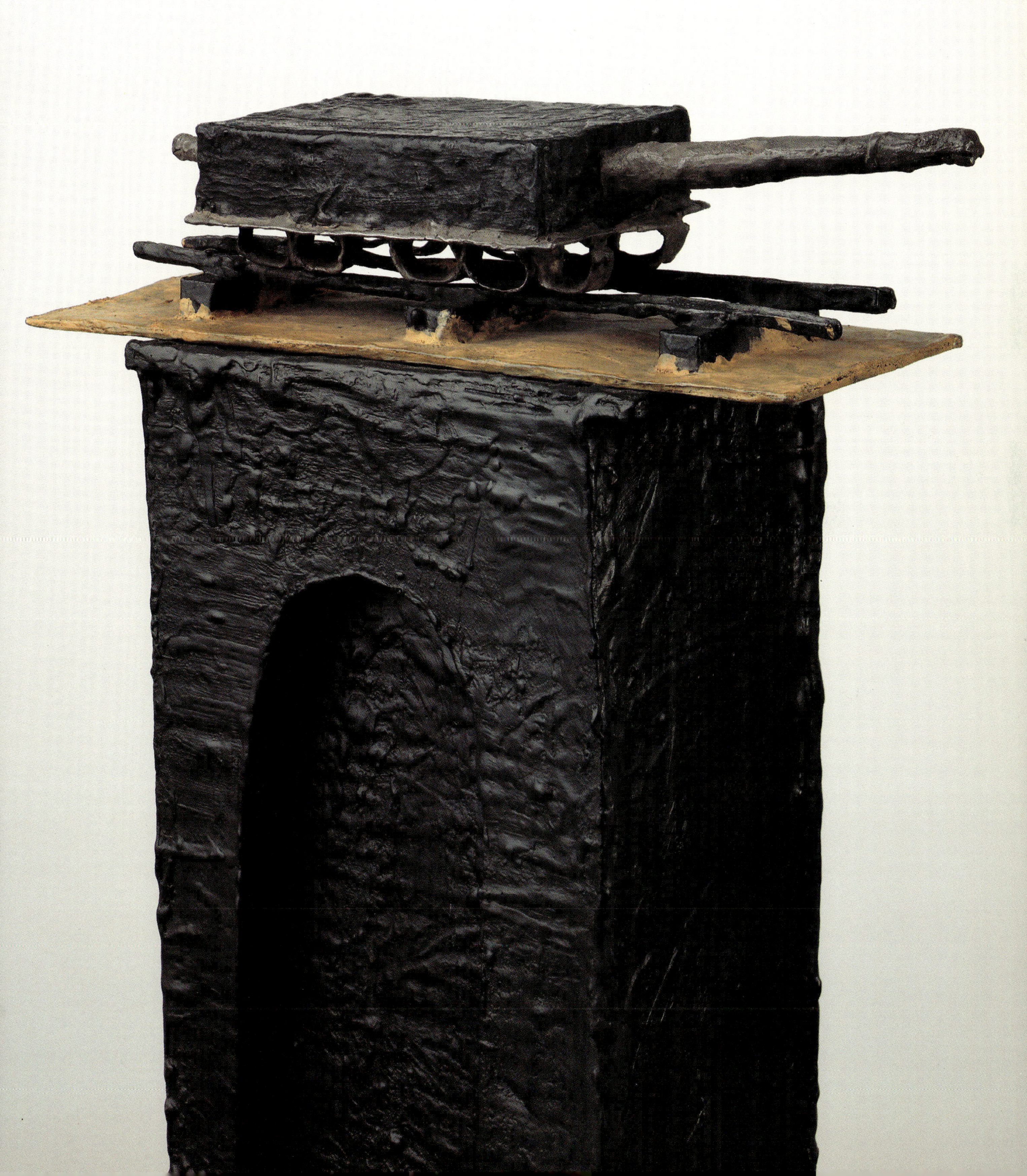

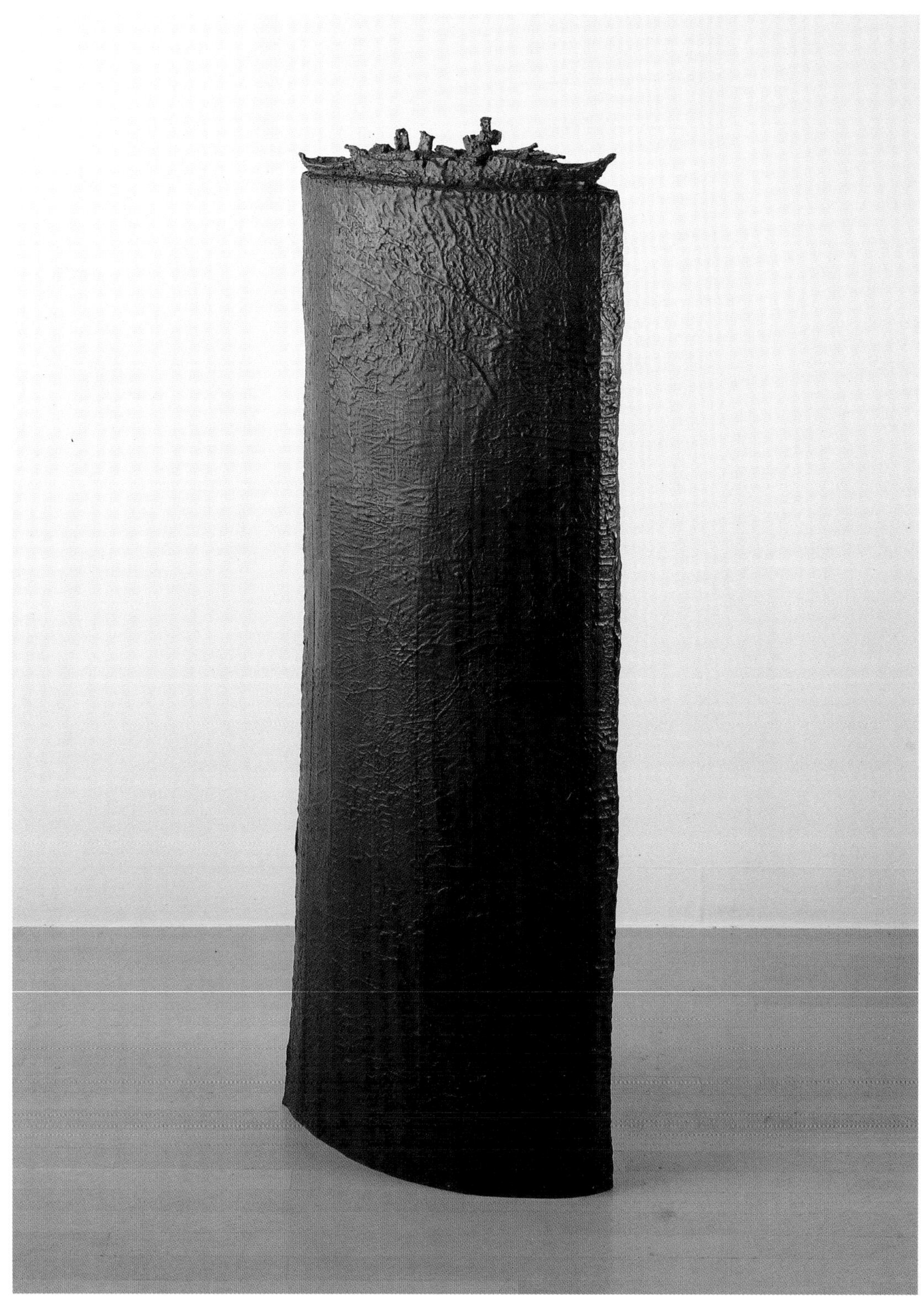

Navy
1990
Patinated bronze
56 x 21 x 8¼ inches
Edition of six

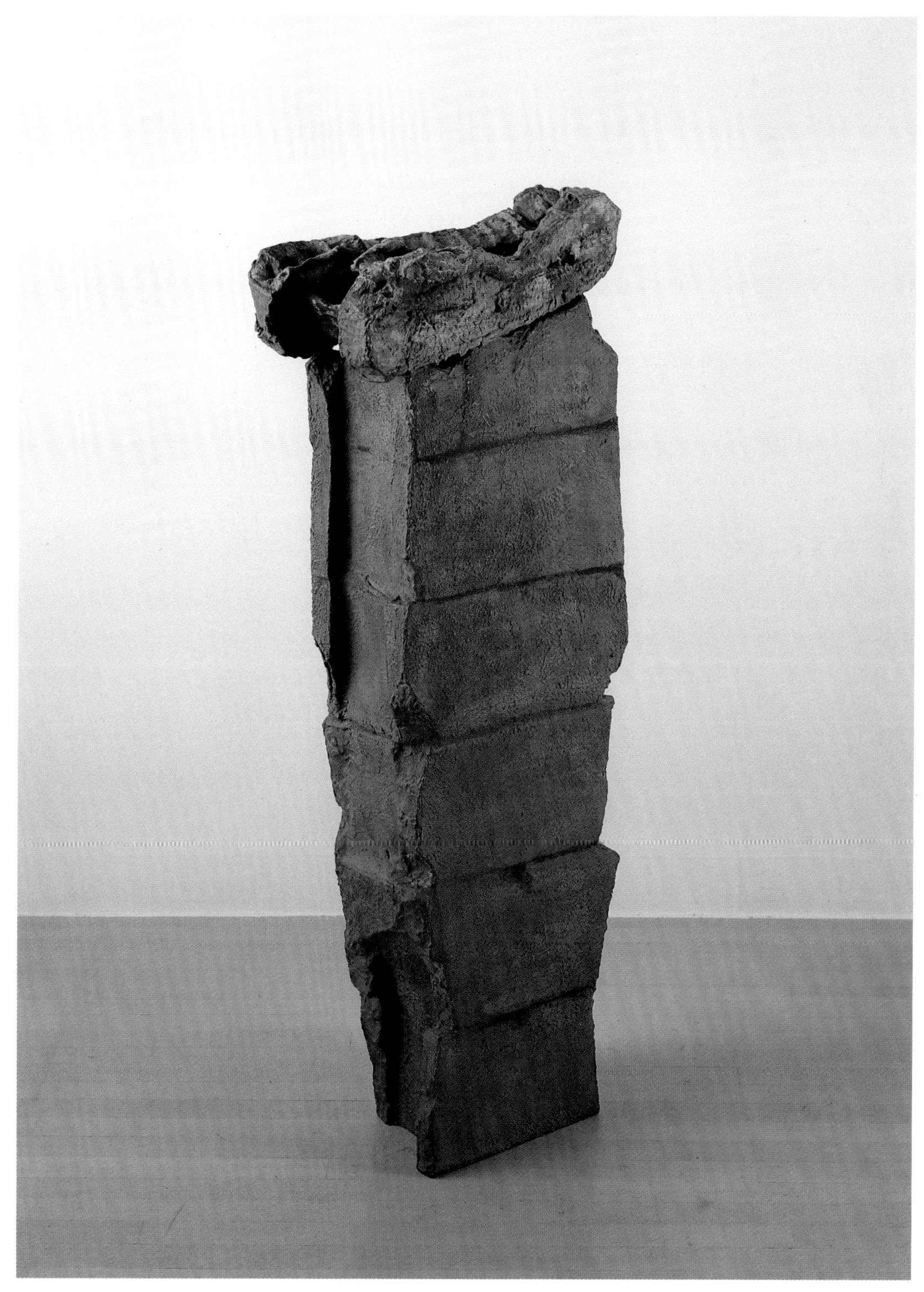

The Chariot of Darius II
1990
Patinated bronze
51½ x 20 x 11½ inches
Edition of six

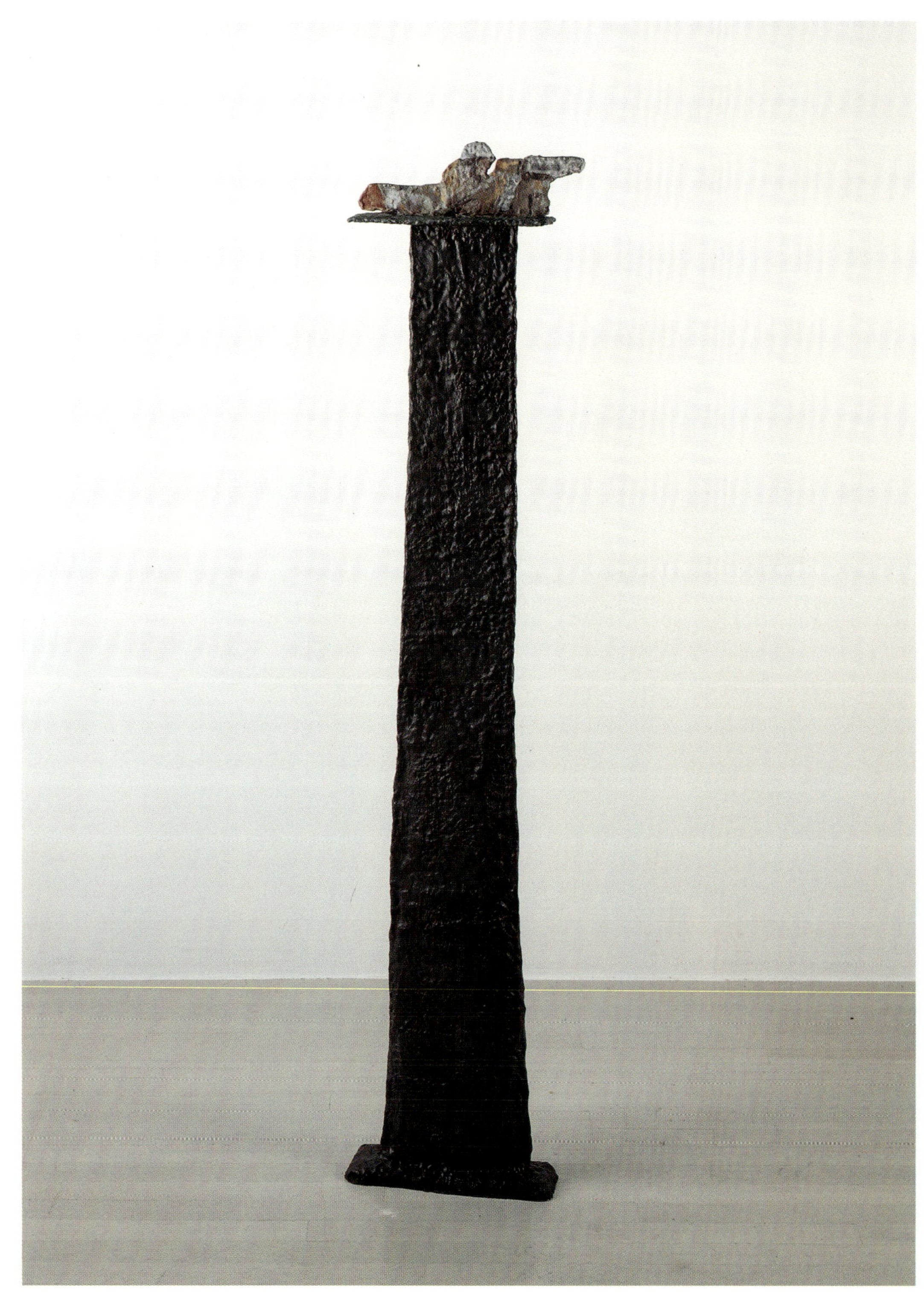

Sighting Down II
1989
Patinated bronze
57¾ x 15 x 3¾ inches
Edition of six

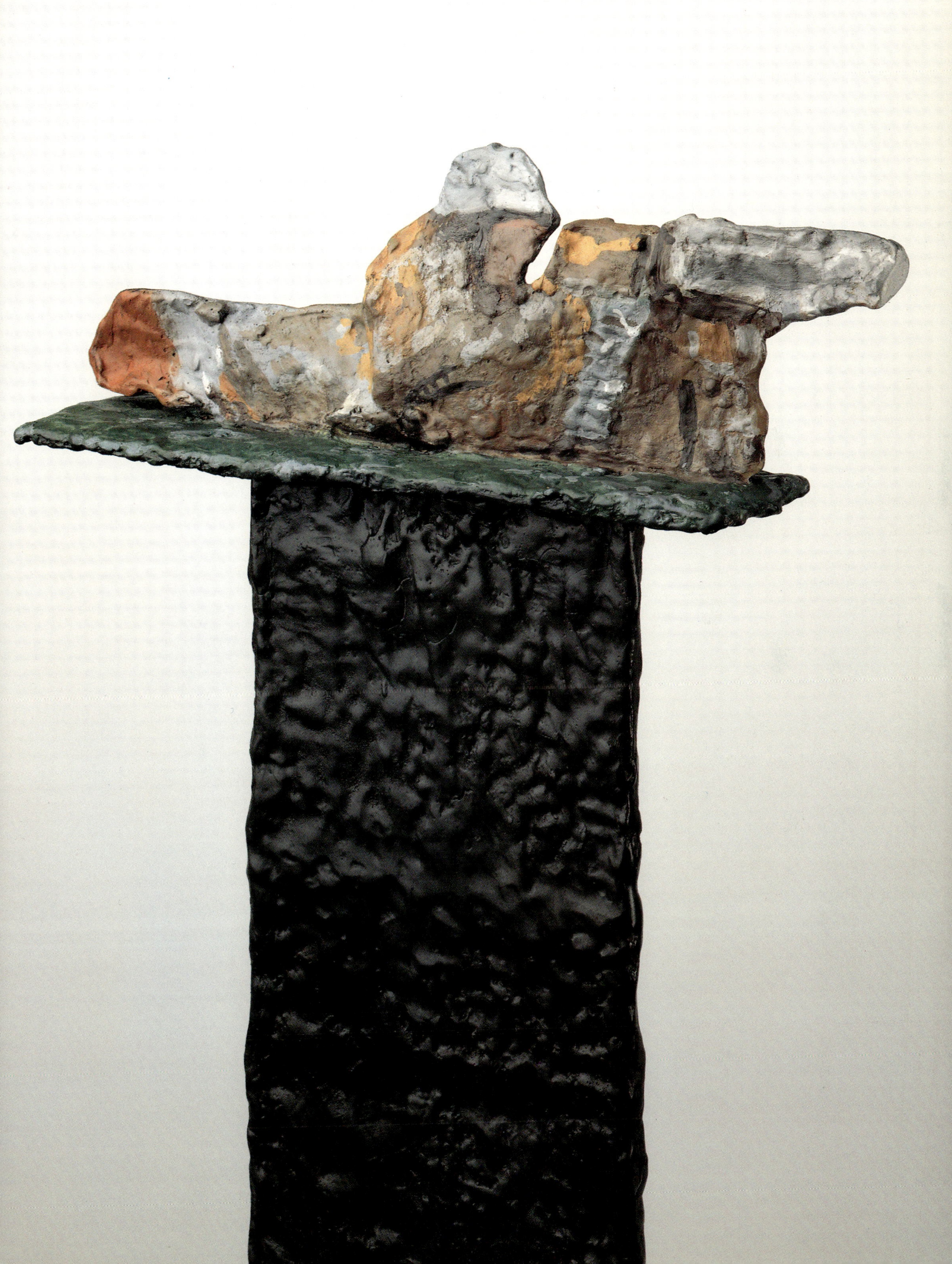

WATERCOLOURS

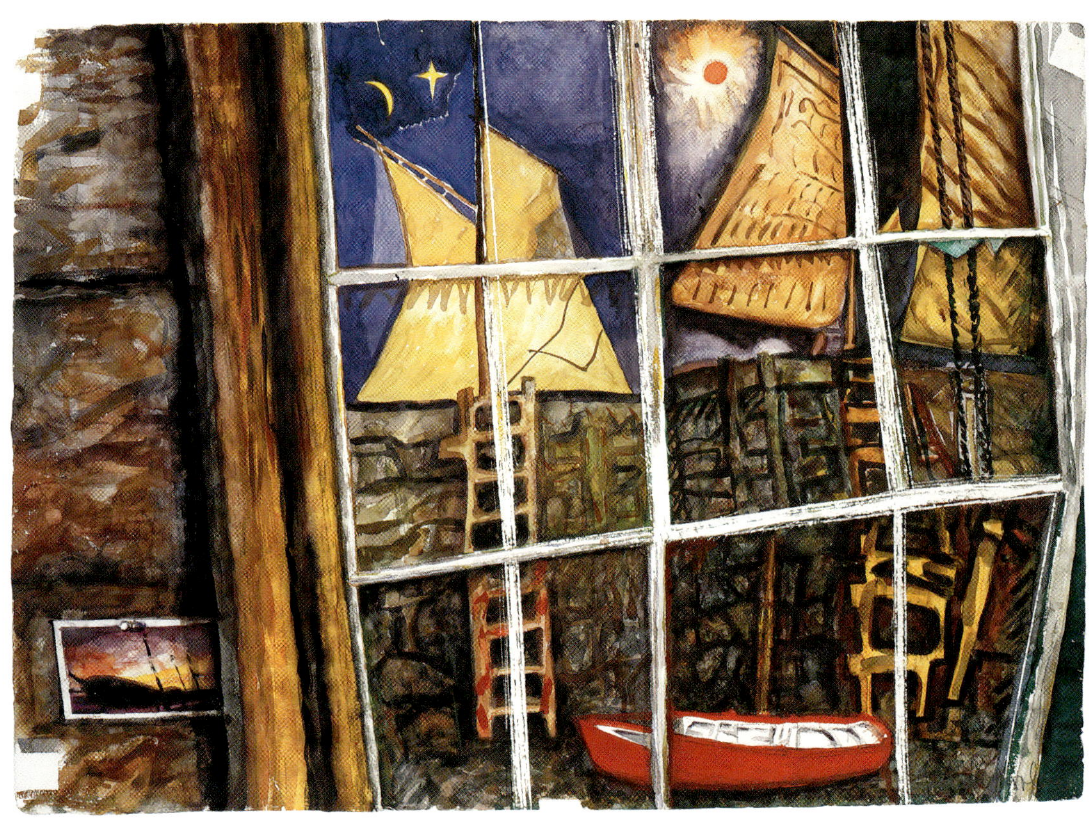

Port Clyde Dreamscape
1989
Watercolour on paper
22 x 30 inches

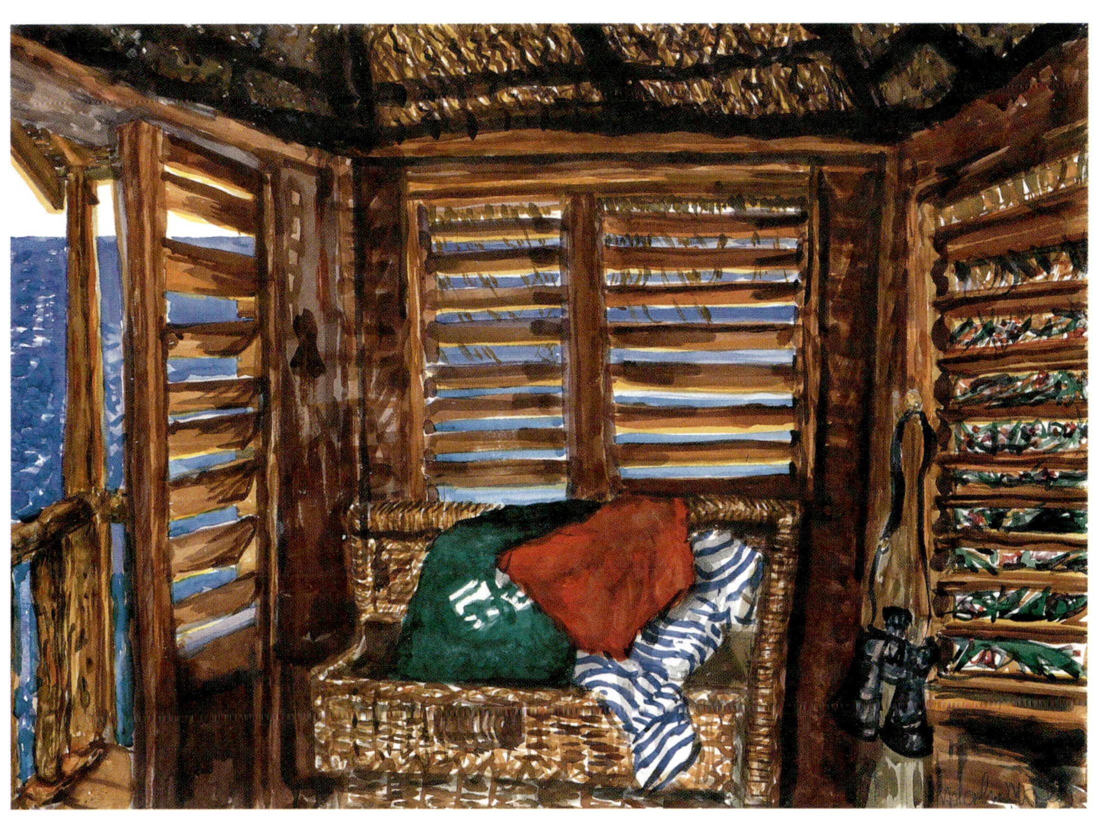

Our Room, Tensing Penn Jamaica
1990
Watercolour on paper
22 x 30 inches

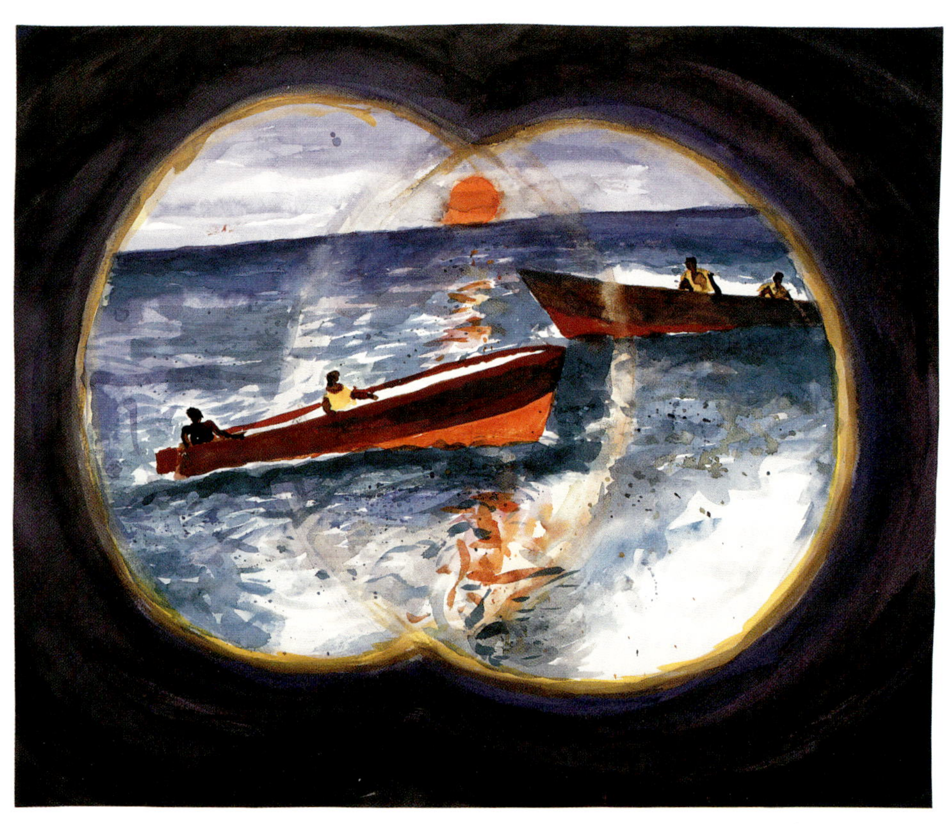

Jamaican Fishermen through the Binox
1990
Watercolour on paper
17¼ x 20 inches

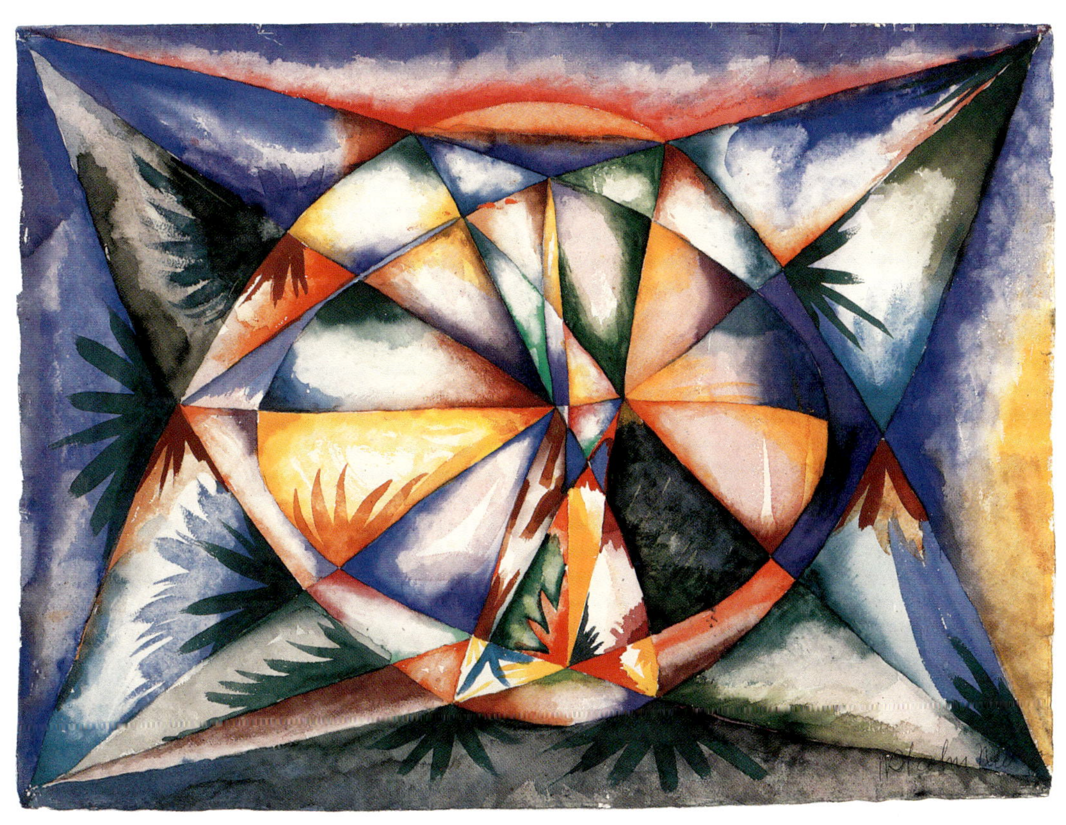

Wigwam
1989
Watercolour on paper
22 x 30 inches

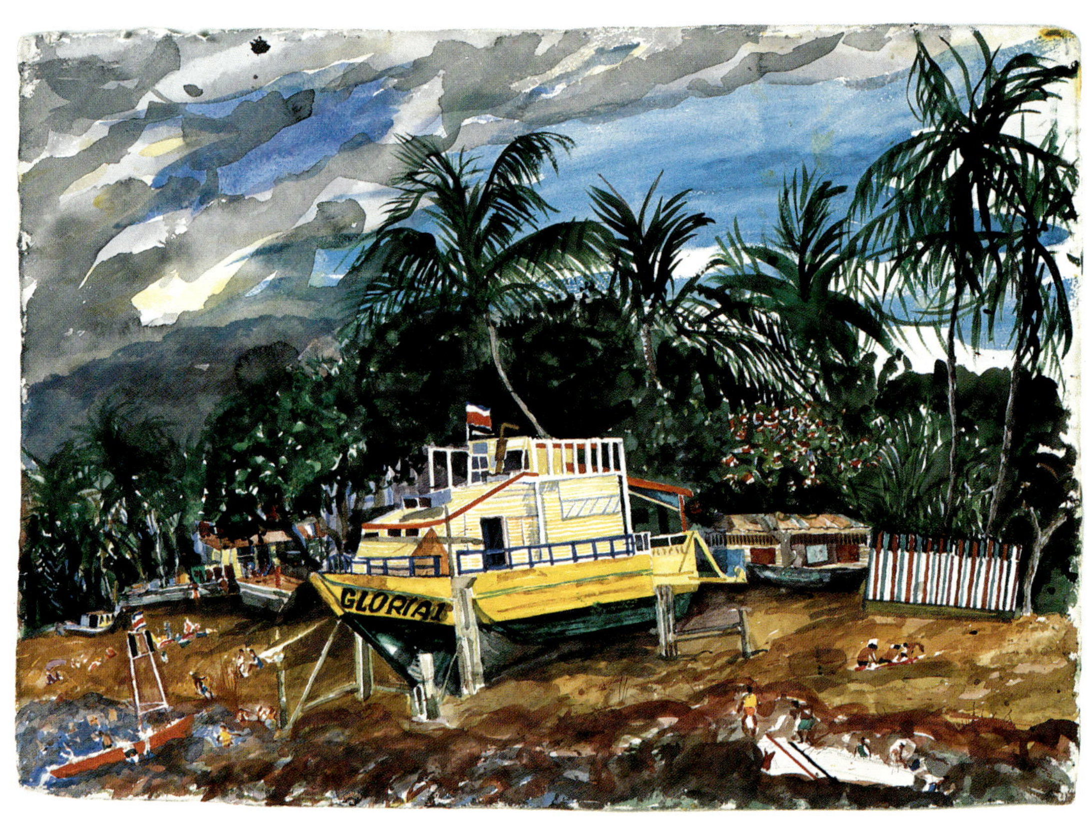

Gloria I
1988-89
Watercolour on paper
22¾ x 30¾ inches

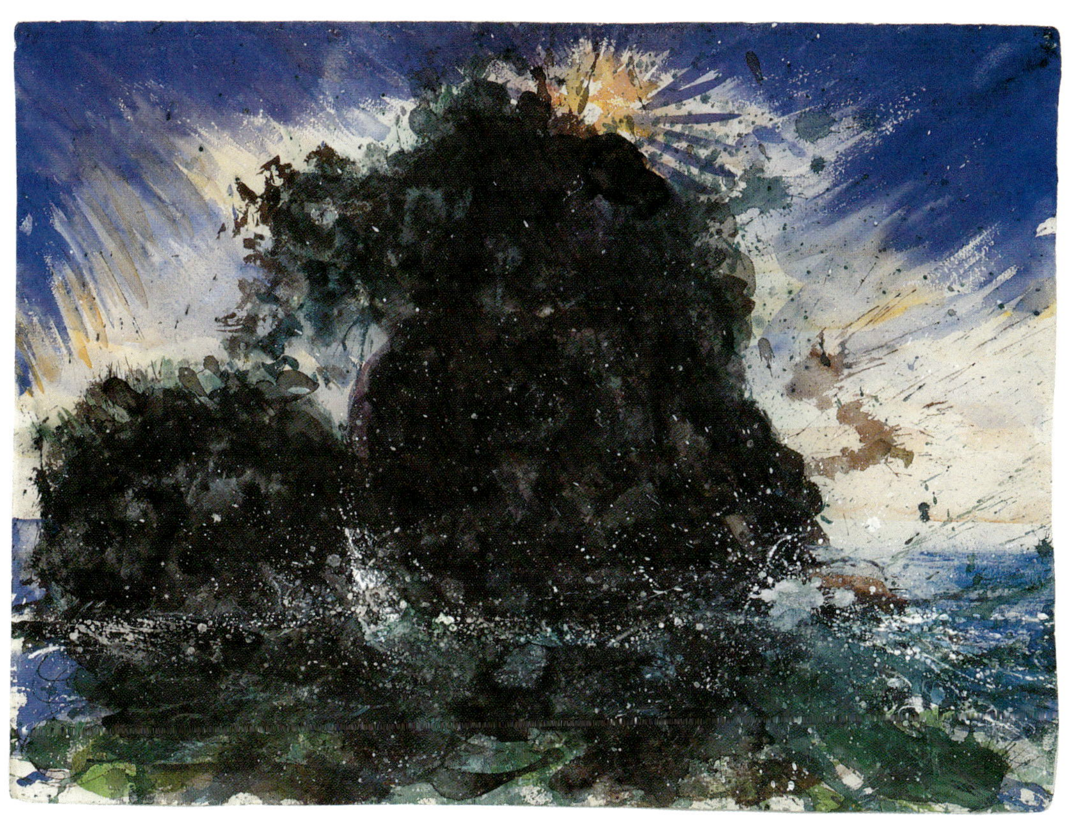

Costa Rica Rockscape
1988-89
Watercolour on paper
22 x 28½ inches

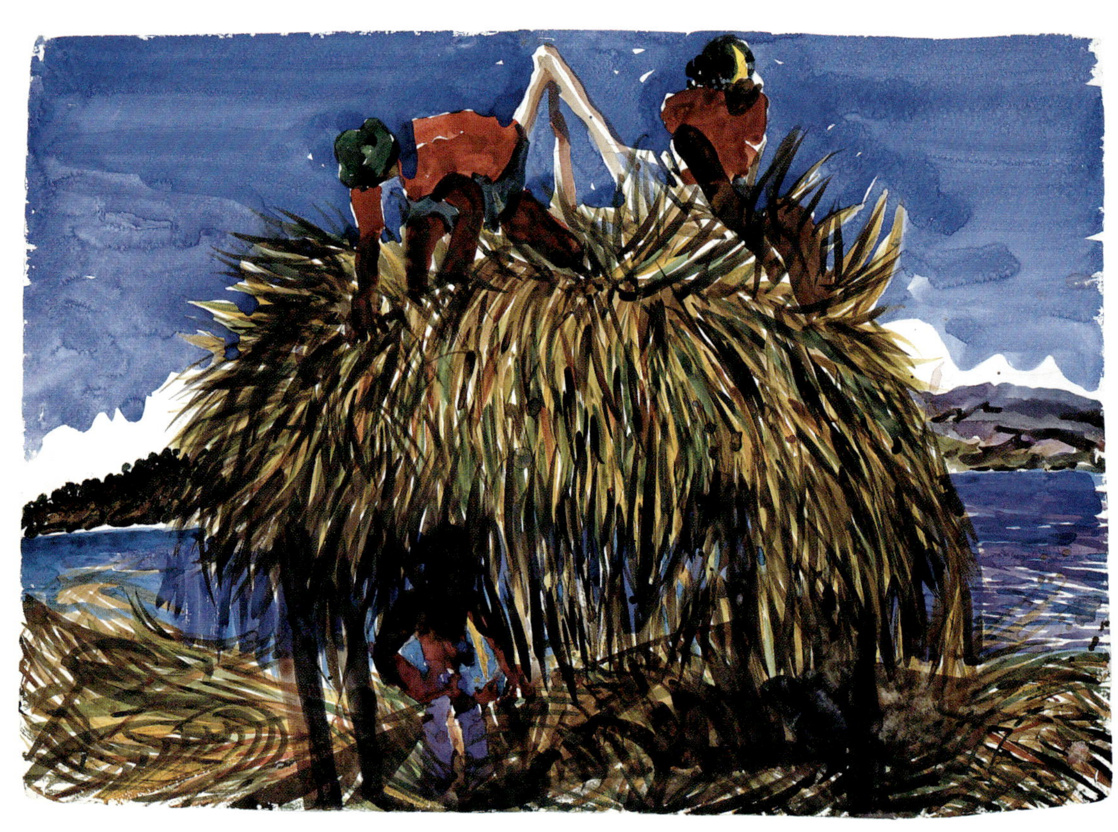

El Palenque
1988-89
Watercolour on paper
22½ x 30¾ inches

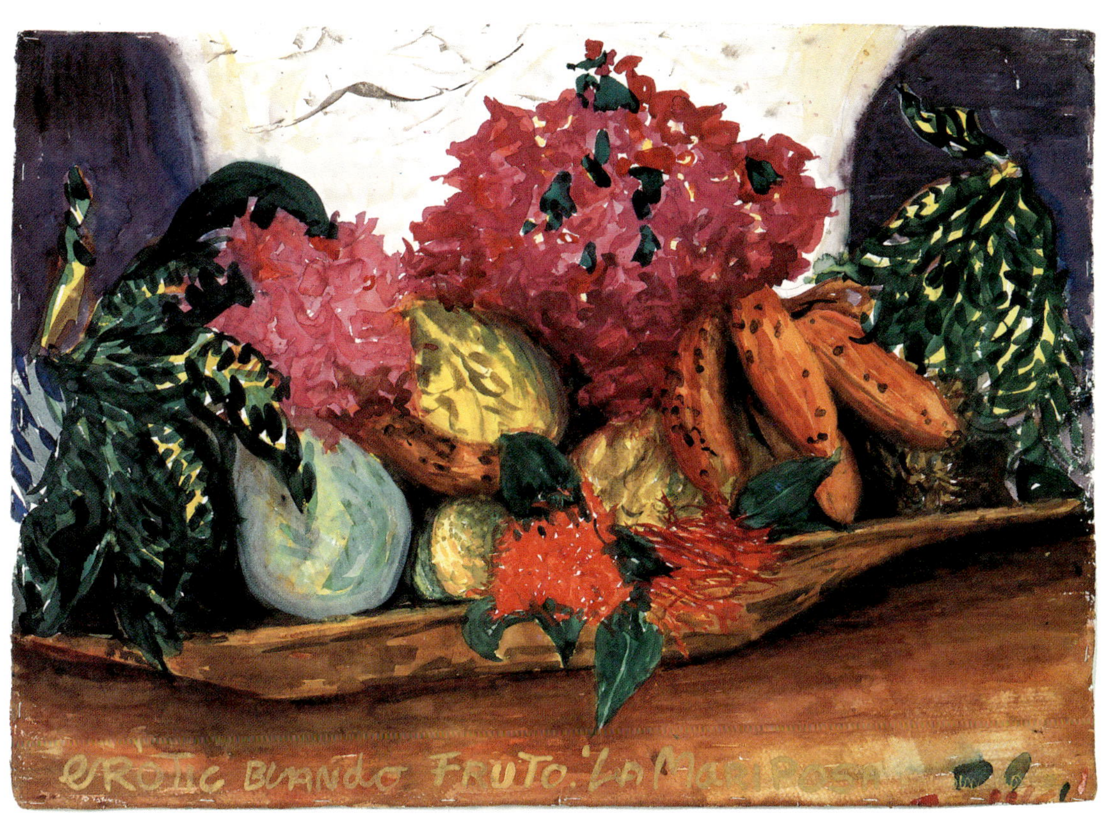

Erotic Blando Fruto: La Mariposa
1988-89
Watercolour on paper
22½ x 30¾ inches

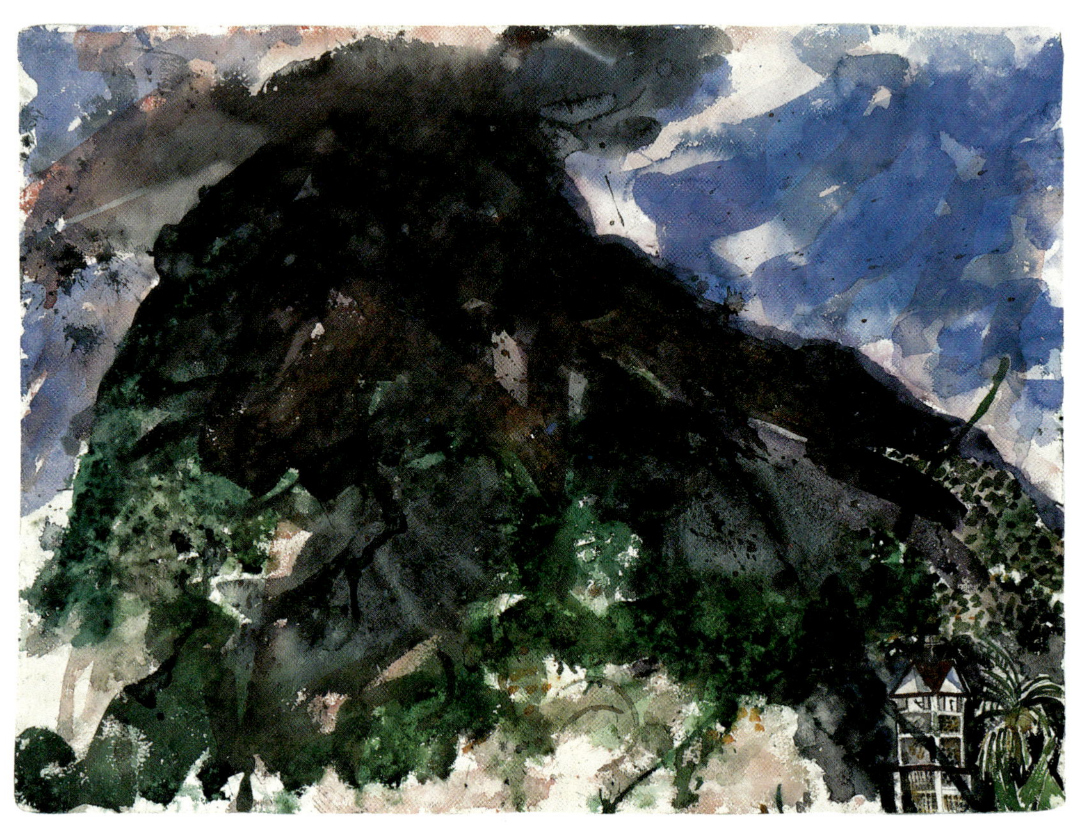

Volcano Arenal
1988-89
Watercolour on paper
21¾ x 28½ inches

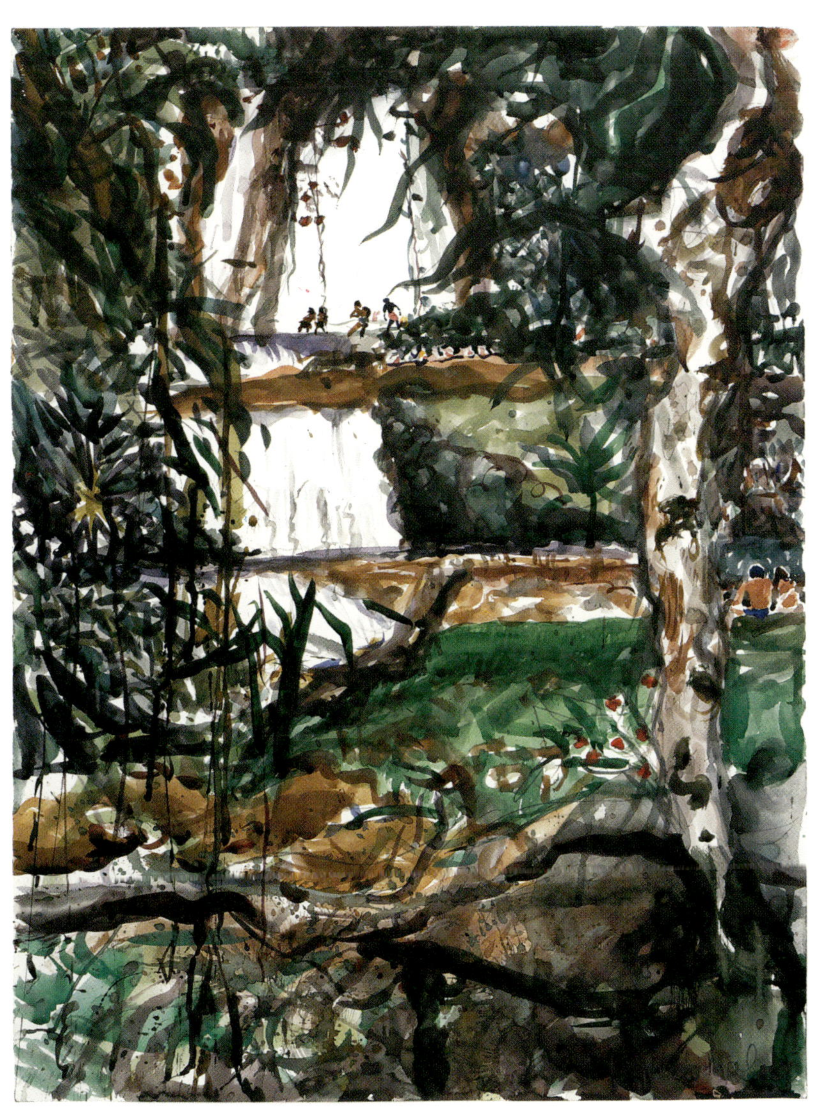

YZ Falls Jamaica
1990
Watercolour on paper
30 x 22 inches

BIOGRAPHY

1931	Born in London.
1953	Graduates from Camberwell School of Arts and Crafts, London.
1957	Graduates from Royal College of Art, London; degree: ARCA (Associate of the Royal College of Art).
1958	Moves to New York.
1965-66	Associate Professor, Ohio State University, Columbus.
1967-69	Instructor, School of Visual Arts, New York.
1972-74	Associate Professor, State University of New York, Stony Brook.
1984	Awarded the First Annual Turner Prize, Tate Gallery, London.

One Man Exhibitions

1957	Kornblee Gallery, New York.
1964	Kornblee Gallery, New York.
1967	Kornblee Gallery, New York.
1969	Kornblee Gallery, New York.
1973	Stefanotty Gallery, New York.
1974	Stefanotty Gallery, New York.
	Galerie Gerald Piltzer, Paris.
1976	Clocktower Gallery, Institute for Art and Urban Resources, New York.
1979	Nancy Hoffman Gallery, New York.
1980	*Matrix 54*, Wadsworth Atheneum, Hartford, Connecticut.
1981	*New Paintings and Watercolours*, Xavier Fourcade, Inc., New York.
1981-82	*Malcolm Morley: Paintings*, Akron Art Museum, Ohio.

1982   *Malcolm Morley: New Work*, Xavier Fourcade, Inc., New York.

1983-84   *Malcolm Morley*, a retrospective exhibition organized by the
            Whitechapel Art Gallery, London. Travels to Kunsthalle Basel,
            Museum Boymans-van Beuningen, Rotterdam, Whitechapel Art
            Gallery, London, Corcoran Gallery of Art, Washington, D.C.,
            Museum of Contemporary Art, Chicago, The Brooklyn Museum,
            New York.

1984   *Malcolm Morley: New Paintings, Watercolours and Prints*, Xavier
            Fourcade, Inc., New York.

            Malcolm Morley: Watercolours, Drawings and Graphics, Ponova
            Gallery, Inc., Toronto.

            Malcolm Morley: Aquarelle, Zeichnungen und Farbradierungen,
            Galerie Nicoline Pon, Zurich.

1985   *Malcolm Morley*, Fabian Carlsson Gallery, London.

1986   *Malcolm Morley: New Paintings and Watercolours 1984-1986*,
            Xavier Fourcade, Inc., New York.

1986-87   *Malcolm Morley: Prints and Process*, Pace Prints, New York.

1988   *Malcolm Morley: Recent Drawings, Lithographs and Watercolours*,
            Temperance Hall Gallery, Bellport, New York.

1988-89   *Malcolm Morley: New Work*, The Pace Gallery, New York.

1990   *Malcolm Morley*, Anthony d'Offay Gallery, London.

1990-91   *Malcolm Morley Watercolours*, organized by the Tate Gallery
            Liverpool. Travels to Bonnefantenmuseum, Maastricht, Kunsthalle
            Basel, Tate Gallery Liverpool and Parrish Art Museum,
            Southampton, Long Island.

ACKNOWLEDGEMENTS

This exhibition, two years in the making, would not have been possible without the unfailing help of the artist. We would like to express our gratitude to both Malcolm and Lida Morley for their generous commitment to this project. We are equally indebted to David Sylvester for his essay and interview, and to Sarah Whitfield for her editorial assistance on these texts. Arnold Glimcher, Douglas Baxter and the staff of The Pace Gallery have given invaluable advice and assistance throughout the preparation of this exhibition —we are deeply grateful to them all. Thanks also to Timothy Greenfield-Sanders for his portrait photograph of the artist, and to the Metropolitan Museum of Art for permission to reproduce *Merrymakers at Shrovetide* by Frans Hals.

Exhibition 11 September to 12 October 1990

Anthony d'Offay Gallery   Dering Street   London W1
Tel 071-499 4100   Fax 071-493 4443

ISBN 0 947564 32 2

Coordinated by Robert Violette and designed by Bailey & Kenny
Printed by Dr. Cantz'sche Druckerei, Stuttgart

BLACK RAINBOW OVER OEDIPUS AT THEBES LOBSTERS FISHING M
EN EROTIC BLANDO FRUTO THE FLYING DUTCHMAN GLORIA SE
NTINEL SIGHTING DOWN I MARKER WHIPPET MARAUDER THE C
HARIOT OF DARIUS II NAVY SIGHTING DOWN II PORT CLYDE DRE
AMSCAPE OUR ROOM, TENSING PENN JAMAICA JAMAICAN FISHER
MEN THROUGH THE BINOX WIGWAM GLORIA I COSTA RICA ROCK
SCAPE EL PALENQUE EROTIC BLANDO FRUTO: LA MARIPOSA VOL
CANO ARENAL YZ FALLS JAMAICA BLACK RAINBOW OVER OEDIP
US AT THEBES LOBSTERS FISHING MEN EROTIC BLANDO FRUTO T
HE FLYING DUTCHMAN GLORIA SENTINEL SIGHTING DOWN I M
ARKER WHIPPET MARAUDER THE CHARIOT OF DARIUS II NAVY S
IGHTING DOWN II PORT CLYDE DREAMSCAPE OUR ROOM, TENSIN
G PENN JAMAICA JAMAICAN FISHERMEN THROUGH THE BINOX W
IGWAM GLORIA I COSTA RICA ROCKSCAPE EL PALENQUE EROTIC
BLANDO FRUTO: LA MARIPOSA VOLCANO ARENAL YZ FALLS JAM
AICA BLACK RAINBOW OVER OEDIPUS AT THEBES LOBSTERS FISH
NG MEN EROTIC BLANDO FRUTO THE FLYING DUTCHMAN GLOR
A SENTINEL SIGHTING DOWN I MARKER WHIPPET MARAUDER T
HE CHARIOT OF DARIUS II NAVY SIGHTING DOWN II PORT CLYDE
DREAMSCAPE OUR ROOM, TENSING PENN JAMAICA JAMAICAN F
SHERMEN THROUGH THE BINOX WIGWAM GLORIA I COSTA RICA
ROCKSCAPE EL PALENQUE EROTIC BLANDO FRUTO: LA MARIPOSA
VOLCANO ARENAL YZ FALLS JAMAICA BLACK RAINBOW OVER OE
DIPUS AT THEBES LOBSTERS FISHING MEN EROTIC BLANDO FRUT
O THE FLYING DUTCHMAN GLORIA SENTINEL SIGHTING DOWN
MARKER WHIPPET MARAUDER THE CHARIOT OF DARIUS II NAVY
SIGHTING DOWN II PORT CLYDE DREAMSCAPE OUR ROOM, TENS
NG PENN JAMAICA JAMAICAN FISHERMEN THROUGH THE BINOX
WIGWAM GLORIA I COSTA RICA ROCKSCAPE EL PALENQUE EROT
C BLANDO FRUTO: LA MARIPOSA VOLCANO ARENAL YZ FALLS JA
MAICA BLACK RAINBOW OVER OEDIPUS AT THEBES LOBSTERS FIS
HING MEN EROTIC BLANDO FRUTO THE FLYING DUTCHMAN GLO
RIA SENTINEL SIGHTING DOWN I MARKER WHIPPET MARAUDER
THE CHARIOT OF DARIUS II NAVY SIGHTING DOWN II PORT CLYD
E DREAMSCAPE OUR ROOM, TENSING PENN JAMAICA JAMAICAN
ISHERMEN THROUGH THE BINOX WIGWAM GLORIA I COSTA RICA
ROCKSCAPE EL PALENQUE EROTIC BLANDO FRUTO: LA MARIPOSA
VOLCANO ARENAL YZ FALLS JAMAICA BLACK RAINBOW OVER OE
DIPUS AT THEBES LOBSTERS FISHING MEN EROTIC BLANDO FRUT
O THE FLYING DUTCHMAN GLORIA SENTINEL SIGHTING DOWN
MARKER WHIPPET MARAUDER THE CHARIOT OF DARIUS II NAVY